Prove It!

Using Textual Evidence

Levels 6–8

MW00560778

Name _____ Date _____   **LESSON 1**

"Should Fidget Spinners Be Banned from Schools?"

Directions: Read the passage. Then, answer the questions.

Should Fidget Spinners Be Banned from Schools? by Jay Heller

Fidget spinners are toys created by Catherine Hettinger that experts claim to help students at school. They have a bearing in the middle, the central axis, then spin with anywhere from three to six prongs that stick out from the center by relying on equal weight distribution. Kids love to "spin" these, but should they be allowed in schools or not? This toy has been advertised as a way to provide many therapeutic benefits by helping students increase focus and concentration and also reducing stress and fidgeting at school, and many students testify that these claims are true, stating that school was easier when they could spin a fidget spinner in class. Fidget spinners claim to help kids with ADHD, autism, and anxiety by providing soothing sensory stimulation. But many teachers and princip... "toys" that are not allowed at school and they are no different than any other t... nothing more than a distraction. Students counter this argument, stating that t... can be used inconspicuously at their desks. However, who would be determined to be fit to b... one to school? There's no way to tell, so many schools have just banned them completely.

1. Underline the text that would be best to use as ... the follow... type of kids do fidget spinner claim to help?"

2. Highlight the text that would be best to use a... paper reasons fidget spinners should be allowe...

Directions: Write *True* or *False* next to each statement about text eviden...

_____ 1. Text evidence can be used to help answer questions in rea... support to a writing topic.

_____ 2. In-text citations are required every time you write.

_____ 3. Paraphrasing means that you write someone else... them credit.

_____ 4. Direct quotations are exact words used as support.

_____ 5. An example of plagiarism would be copying two sentences ... wrote on the Internet and making it seem like you were th... words by not having an in-text citation.

Tip: Text evidence should prove exactly what it is you are try... carefully chosen words that match your question or topic exactly.

© Shell Education

Introduction

Body of Content

Conclusion

Melissa Cheesman Smith
Terri Schilling
Foreword by Alan Sitomer

Publishing Credits

Corinne Burton, M.A.Ed., *Publisher*; Conni Medina, M.A.Ed., *Managing Editor*; Emily R. Smith, M.A.Ed., *Content Director*; Veronique Bos, *Creative Director*; Shaun N. Bernadou, *Art Director*; Stephanie Bernard, *Associate Editor*; Courtney Roberson, *Senior Graphic Designer*

Image Credits

All images from Shutterstock except p.88 (bottom), p.89 (all), p.91, p.94, p.106 (bottom) iStock

Standards

© 2014 Mid-continent Research for Education and Learning
© Copyright 2010. National Governors Association Center for Best Practices and Council of Chief State School Officers. All rights reserved.
© Copyright 2007–2017 Texas Education Association (TEA). All rights reserved.
ISTE Standards for Students, ©2016, ISTE® (International Society for Technology in Education), iste.org. All rights reserved.
© 2007 Teachers of English to Speakers of Other Languages, Inc. (TESOL)
© 2014 Board of Regents of the University of Wisconsin System, on behalf of the WIDA—www.wida.us

Shell Education

A division of Teacher Created Materials
5301 Oceanus Drive
Huntington Beach, CA 92649-1030

www.tcmpub.com/shell-education

ISBN 978-1-4258-1701-5

©2018 Shell Educational Publishing, Inc.

Table of Contents

From the Authors

Dedication

I dedicate this book to Deb Junkes for being my cheerleader in publication before I even knew I could play.—M.C.S.

I dedicate this book to Michael Schilling for always believing in me and giving me guidance and reassurance when I needed it most.—T.S

About Us

Terri Schilling, M.Ed., has a master's degree in educational leadership along with a reading specialist endorsement. She has been teaching for 15 years and presents at literacy professional development workshops.

Melissa Cheesman Smith, M.Ed., holds a master's degree in curriculum and instruction and has been teaching for 10 years. She teaches literacy classes for a university, presents at literacy conferences, and facilitates professional development workshops.

Acknowledgments

We would like to thank our editors and production team at Teacher Created Materials, namely Emily Smith and Stephanie Bernard, for taking our simple idea and crafting it into an easy-to-use resource for teachers. We'd also like to acknowledge Courtney Roberson for the beautiful cover and interior design of the book.

We'd like to thank Teacher Created Materials for believing that the teachers in the trenches are the root and heart of curriculum design, allowing resources to be produced from the ground up to create material that works for teachers to teach and students to learn.

From Melissa: I would like to thank my husband, David, and family for the extra time it took out of our family time to work on the book and for allowing me the time to develop trainings for teachers around the ideas based in this resource. I would especially like to thank my coauthor, Terri. As a friend and colleague, I have both love and respect for Terri as a friend and as a lifelong learner who inspires me to be a better teacher and push myself. "A friend is someone who knows all about you and still loves you."—Elbert Hubbard

From Terri: Thank you to Kete, Lisa, Dillon, and Autry for always bringing out the best in me; without all of you, I never could have followed my dreams. I am particularly appreciative to Melissa for asking me to partner with her in writing this book. It has been a rewarding experience following the process and learning from Melissa along the way. We have spent many years together growing as teachers and friends, of which I am truly grateful.

The Importance of Evidence

We live in a world where evidence is more important than ever. With people asserting all sorts of claims (i.e., "Believe me!", "No, believe me!", "No, don't believe either of those ding-dongs… BELIEVE ME!") in all sorts of formats (i.e., print, online, social media, television), the student who does not own the skill of cool, detached, reasoned, discernment is a student ill-prepared to face the demands of modern life.

Quite simply, the ability to understand and critically analyze evidence is the foremost key to avoid being duped (in a world filled with dupers). This is why I am such a fan of the Prove It! series. Melissa Cheesman Smith and Terri Schilling do not want students passively accepting assertions; they insist today's learners develop investigative eyes when it comes to analyzing contentions. Their work focuses on asking students to probe deeper, think critically, and get to the core of WHY a claim ought to be believed. Their work promotes meritocracy— the best ideas supported by the most convincing evidence wins. Forget the cult of personality. Throw away the unsupportable, inflammatory claims. Simply provide concrete, logical evidence to support your points, and the rest will take care of itself. In order to sustain a well-informed democracy, this is no small matter.

All in all, I love how this series rests on the foundation of knowing that reading requires students not to just form opinions about the text, but rather USE the text to form educated responses. That's a BIG WIN! From the embedded academic vocabulary instruction, to teaching students what credible and reliable sources are (so they can learn how to critically think and make informed decisions), to text structure and inferences, and on and on, there are many wonderful resources made available. And with such a well-organized progression of instruction, it's hard not to smile when you take a gander at all the goodies being offered.

As we all know, there is a sea change afoot in education. Evidence-based analysis is no longer something left for college-level instruction as students as young as seven years old are being asked to cite evidence to support their claims. To that end, materials that make weighty concepts accessible to young learners are essential. Do yourself a favor and allow expert educators to help connect the dots from assertions to evidence through a user-friendly set of instructional tools built specifically for the modern classroom. This Prove It! series rocks!

—Alan Lawrence Sitomer
California Teacher of the Year Award Winner
Author: *Mastering Short Response: Claim It! Cite It! Cement It!* by Scholastic

Using Textual Evidence and Citations

Instructionally, reading and writing change as they parallel the technological demands of the generation. Today, students must be able to write for purpose and with intent when conveying information on a topic, whether informational or argumentative, and they must be able to use printed text with an Internet technology base to back up that information. Providing purpose is essential for students because "sometimes our students' purposes don't match up with the purposes set for them to achieve in school" (Atkins 2011). We have to help set the purpose of success. To have purpose and intent, research on a topic is essential. The purpose of using text evidence is to teach students habits of argument. As Douglas Fisher and Nancy Frey point out, "students have to develop habits that allow them to mine texts for details, ideas, and deeper meanings" (2014, 4).

When finding evidence, students must learn how to cite textual evidence not only as a basic matter of research, but also as a way to validate their own statements and thinking through evidence-based arguments. When using textual evidence, a quotation or paraphrased text with an in-text citation is essential. While students may not need to formally conform to one specific style (MLA *or* APA), a basic in-text citation is required when quoting or paraphrasing text. This book will introduce students to best practices in citation formatting that can be used throughout elementary and middle school until they are required to learn certain styles in high school and college. For our purposes, MLA style will be used, as elementary and middle school students are more likely to be engaged in using page numbers from a given text rather than finding their own research.

Using textual evidence and citations is imperative for advancing through college and career readiness standards and also for college itself. Students will need this skill most directly for high-stakes testing, as much of the literacy testing (both reading and writing) today revolves around text-based evidence or document-based questions (DBQs). There is a direct connection between reading and writing when using text evidence and students having the ability to analyze text. Research shows that having students write an extended analytical response supported with text evidence and explanation has a positive impact on reading comprehension (Graham and Hebert 2010). Students will be required to use this skill for authoring papers in high school, in college, and possibly in their careers.

Students must learn how to read critically in literary and informational texts, looking for central ideas to comprehend and research. So much of what we, as adults, process and read each day falls under the writing genres of informational or argumentative. We have to be critical to take in the information, sort it, and use what is credible to make informed decisions and create educated opinions. Douglas Fisher and Nancy Frey note that "understanding the purpose of and how others use evidence, reading closely looking for evidence, and annotating and sourcing texts are important aspects students must learn if they are going to be proficient composers who integrate evidence and respond to complex tasks" (2014, 5).

Using Textual Evidence and Citations *(cont.)*

Writing Genres

Three commonly used nonfiction writing genres today are informational, persuasive, and argumentative. While persuasive and argumentative may at first seem synonymous, as they each state claims, give reasons, and provide evidence, the differences between the two are significant:

- **Persuasive writing** aims to prove a claim through opinion, often through an emotional appeal, followed by personal anecdotes and reasons that may be effective but do not completely verify the claim.

- **Argumentative writing** aims to prove a claim through a series of logical statements, followed by facts, examples, and evidence that is verifiable.

Educators must teach students a unique skill set to help write within these genres using technological demands now required to present information. These skills require students today to be able do the following skills.

Locate Resources

- Question what is found on the Internet, and filter through what is and is not related to the specific topic.

- Know not only how to locate information but how to determine what a credible and reliable source looks like. Know the reason behind why these sources are imperative to use when doing research.

- Understand how to find credible and reliable sources.

Gather Resources

- Use a variety of multimodal sources to thoroughly encompass the totality of the topic researched. Writing is now created in a multimodal fashion. This means that students are no longer simply looking up facts in encyclopedias and regurgitating the information in their own words. The main source of information today is the Internet. Within the Internet, there are videos, news reports, websites, and infographics that provide a variety of ways to research, organize, and write about various topics.

- Find enough evidence to support a solid understanding of the topic, allowing it to be reorganized in a way that will be presentable for the intended audience.

Select and Organize Evidence

- Interpret the text. Read to determine which evidence correlates to the specific reasons, intent, and purpose of the topic.

- Find short, purposeful sections of the text that relate directly to a topic, whether through information or reason.

Write with Purpose and Intent

- Show critical thinking by analyzing the resources found and using in-text citations.

- Cite using paraphrasing.

- Cite using exact quotations.

- Understand the definition and ramifications of plagiarism.

In addition to understanding how to locate sources and gather reliable information, learning how to cite textual evidence is a key component in reading and writing education today.

Textual Evidence Vocabulary

Use text-evidence vocabulary (*citation vs. quotation*) when teaching. Helping students understand the vocabulary will support the content of the lessons and ensure student success in the activities. It may be helpful to review words and phrases specific to textual evidence before beginning the lessons. For easy reference, a text evidence vocabulary chart is included on page 127.

In-Text Citations in Reading

Students must learn how to read critically in literary and informational texts through close reading, looking for central ideas to comprehend and research further. Students must be aware that sometimes they "need to read because they will be asked to synthesize information or produce ideas based on evidence" (Fisher and Frey 2014, 2). Students have to be critical to take in information, sort it, and use what is credible to make informed decisions or to create educated opinions. In this product, students will practice such skills by reading pieces of informational text on similar topics. They will closely read and annotate the passages. They will also focus on specific skills within the close reading to enhance their annotation skills. Students will answer comprehension questions and cite textual evidence in their answers. A rubric for close-reading annotations is provided on page 130.

In-Text Citations in Writing

It is critical for students to learn to write using more than their opinions as support. Students should also learn to determine their intended audience as well as decide on the purpose of their writing, because we "organize events, ideas, and arguments in a coherent fashion for a purpose and to meet the needs of an audience" (Fisher and Frey 2014, 10). Students must learn to find relevant and credible sources, decipher what information is relevant to their topic, and use evidence from the text to support their explanations. In this resource, the reading passages are designed to be informational while the writing passages are designed to be argumentative, so students can logically use textual evidence in their writing. Students will be prompted to cite textual evidence to support their responses. A rubric for citing textual evidence in writing prompt is provided on page 131.

How to Use This Book

It is imperative that students receive direct instruction on all the elements of using textual citations. This resource includes everything needed for students to learn basic textual evidence skills in reading and writing. There are four main sections of the book for students to practice all facets of using textual evidence in reading and writing.

Textual Evidence in Reading

Students will answer comprehension questions based on narrative, informative, or argumentative texts. They will cite sources and use paraphrasing or direct quotations, as well as evidence, to prove inferential answers.

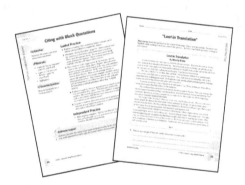

Reading Application Practice

Students will practice close reading passages using annotations strategies, answer questions related to the texts, and practically apply textual evidence with skills learned.

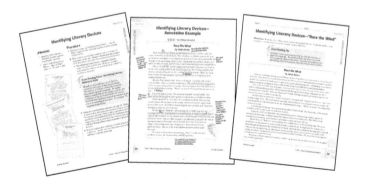

Textual Evidence in Writing

Students will practice gathering and organizing sources and supporting claims with evidence found in the text.

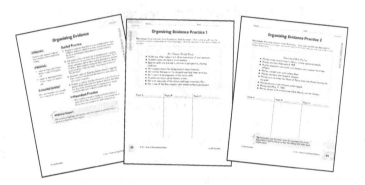

Writing Application Prompts

Students will read passages and be given writing prompts. If directed by the teacher, they can then use the Internet to further research the topics and find additional evidence related to the prompts. Students are asked to use basic writing organization practices of including an introduction, body content, and a conclusion for each written response. Within the prompts, students practically apply their evidence skills learned in the lessons to complete the prompt.

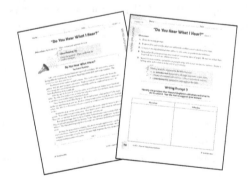

Standards Correlations

Shell Education is committed to producing educational materials that are research and standards based. In this effort, all products are correlated to the academic standards of all 50 United States, the District of Columbia, the Department of Defense Dependent Schools, and all Canadian provinces.

How to Find Standards Correlations

The general standards are provided in the Digital Resources (standards.pdf). Or, to print a customized correlation report of this product for your state, visit our website at **www.tcmpub. com/administrators/correlations/** and follow the on-screen directions. If you require assistance in printing correlation reports, please contact Customer Service at 1-800-777-3450.

Purpose and Intent of Standards

The Every Student Succeeds Act (ESSA) mandates that all states adopt challenging academic standards that help students meet the goal of college and career readiness. While many states had already adopted academic standards prior to ESSA, the act continues to hold states accountable for detailed and comprehensive standards.

Standards are designed to focus instruction and guide adoption of curricula. Standards are statements that describe the criteria necessary for students to meet specific academic goals. They define the knowledge, skills, and content students should acquire at each level. Standards are also used to develop standardized tests to evaluate students' academic progress.

Teachers are required to demonstrate how their lessons meet state standards. State standards are used in development of all of our products, so educators can be assured they meet the academic requirements of each state.

College and Career Readiness Standards

Today's College and Career Readiness (CCR) standards offer guidelines for preparing K–12 students with the knowledge and skills that are necessary to succeed in postsecondary job training and education. CCR standards include the Common Core State Standards (CCSS) as well as other state-adopted standards such as the Texas Essential Knowledge and Skills (TEKS) and the Virginia Standards of Learning (SOL). The CCR standards listed on page 14 support the objectives presented throughout the lessons.

McREL Compendium

Each year, McREL analyzes state standards and revises the compendium to produce a general compilation of national standards. The standards listed on page 13 support the objectives presented throughout the lessons.

TESOL and WIDA Standards

The lessons in this book promote English language development for English language learners.

ISTE Standards

The International Society for Technology in Education (ISTE) standards provide guidelines for the knowledge and skills needed to succeed in the twenty-first century.

Standards Correlations *(cont.)*

Literacy Standards

6th Grade	**Reading**	• Cite textual evidence to support analysis of what the text says explicitly as well as inferences drawn from the text.
	Writing	• Use technology, including the Internet, to produce and publish writing as well as to interact and collaborate with others. • Conduct short research projects to answer a question, drawing on several sources and refocusing the inquiry when appropriate. • Gather relevant information from multiple print and digital sources; assess the credibility of each source; and quote or paraphrase the data and conclusions of others while avoiding plagiarism and providing basic bibliographic information for sources. • Draw evidence from literary or informational texts to support analysis, reflection, and research.
7th Grade	**Reading**	• Cite several pieces of textual evidence to support analysis of what the text says explicitly as well as inferences drawn from the text.
	Writing	• Use technology, including the Internet, to produce and publish writing and link to and cite sources as well as to interact and collaborate with others, including linking to and citing sources. • Conduct short research projects to answer a question, drawing on several sources and generating additional related, focused questions for further research and investigation. • Gather relevant information from multiple print and digital sources, using search terms effectively; assess the credibility and accuracy of each source; and quote or paraphrase the data and conclusions of others while avoiding plagiarism and following a standard format for citation. • Draw evidence from literary or informational texts to support analysis, reflection, and research.

Standards Correlations *(cont.)*

8th Grade	**Reading**	• Cite the textual evidence that most strongly supports an analysis of what the text says explicitly as well as inferences drawn from the text.
	Writing	• Use technology, including the Internet, to produce and publish writing and present the relationships between information and ideas efficiently as well as to interact and collaborate with others. • Conduct short research projects to answer a question (including a self-generated question), drawing on several sources and generating additional related, focused questions that allow for multiple avenues of exploration. • Gather relevant information from multiple print and digital sources, using search terms effectively; assess the credibility and accuracy of each source; and quote or paraphrase the data and conclusions of others while avoiding plagiarism and following a standard format for citation. • Draw evidence from literary or informational texts to support analysis, reflection, and research.

51701—Prove It! Using Textual Evidence

Reading Lessons and Application

Textual Evidence in Reading

Reading Application Practice

Introduction to Textual Evidence

🔍 Objective

Students will learn the definitions and uses of textual evidence, quotations, paraphrasing, and in-text citations in academic writing.

✏️ Materials

- copies of *Matching* (page 17; page17.pdf)
- copies of *"My Maiden Voyage"* (page 18; page18.pdf)
- copies of *True/False* (page 19; page19.pdf)
- copies of *"Should Fidget Spinners Be Banned from Schools?"* (page 20; page20.pdf)
- highlighters

💡 Essential Question

How do I use textual evidence to answer questions in reading?

Guided Practice

1. Explain to students the purpose of textual evidence. Tell students, "When we read or write, we often use text to give answers from our reading or form opinions and prove points in writing. When we do this, we use what is called *text evidence*. This means that we use exact words (quotations) or general ideas (paraphrasing) from the text to support the points we are explaining or arguing and then include an in-text citation."

2. Tell students, "When you use someone else's ideas, you have to cite the text. This means you must give credit to the author who originally wrote the text. If you don't, this can be considered plagiarism. Plagiarism is taking someone else's words or thoughts and passing it off as your own. If you plagiarize someone's work, you are infringing on a copyright, which is a protection given to authors for original writing. You do not need to cite if the idea is your own or is common knowledge, but you *do* need to cite if you got the idea or words from another source." It is important to have students understand that in-text citations are used to avoid plagiarism. This can be very important as you are writing papers in higher education, as plagiarism is illegal and can result in negative consequences.

3. Distribute *Matching* (page 17). Work with students to match the vocabulary words to the definitions.

4. Distribute *"My Maiden Voyage,"* (page 18) and read the passage together. Have students choose parts of the text that would be good support for their answers to the reading comprehension question. Finally, help students determine which part of the text would be strong support to prove their points for the writing prompt.

Independent Practice

- Have students complete *True/False* (page 19) and *"Should Fidget Spinners Be Banned from Schools?"* (page 20) in class, as homework, or as assessments to ensure they can complete the skill independently.

Additional Support

Have students annotate each individual sentence, indicating which text relates to each question.

Matching

Directions: Match the words about citing sources to their definitions.

_____ **1.** text

_____ **2.** in-text citation

_____ **3.** plagiarism

_____ **4.** direct quotation

_____ **5.** paraphrasing

a. stating the author and page number from a source when using a direct quotation or paraphrasing

b. restatement or rewording of an idea from a text

c. the exact words of someone else woven into your writing, noted by using quotation marks

d. the original piece of writing being cited

e. the practice of taking someone else's work and passing them off as your own

Directions: In your own words, explain the difference between a direct quotation and paraphrasing.

_____

_____

_____

_____

_____

_____

_____

_____

Name _____ Date _____

"My Maiden Voyage"

Directions: Read the passage. Then, answer the questions.

My Maiden Voyage
by Roberta Maioni

I was carried by a swarm of other passengers to the boat deck and shall never forget the strange sight. There were pieces of ice all over the deck and groups of men and women, looking gaunt and fearful in their night attire or in odd garments hastily donned.

It was bitterly cold. I watched them preparing to lower the lifeboats. I heard the order, "Women and children first." I saw women parting from their husbands and fathers—the women to live and the men to die.

An elderly officer, with tears streaming down his cheeks, helped us into one of the lifeboats. He was Captain Smith—the master of that ill-fated vessel. As the lifeboat began to descend, I thought I heard him say, "Goodbye, remember you are British."

We dropped over 60 feet down the side of that huge vessel. It seemed an eternity before the lifeboat reached the water. When we were at a safe distance, we watched the *Titanic* sink into the black depths.

Then I heard the terrible last cries of the 1,200 men, women, and children left aboard her, rising above the din of the explosion of the boilers. For a moment, the sky was lighted up. We saw that dreadful iceberg in the distance, like some grim monster watching its prey as it dies. Then came the awful silence—more terrible than the sounds that had gone before.

page 1

1. Highlight the text that would be best to use in an informational paper about the feelings of the people on board the *Titanic*.

2. Underline the textual evidence that best answers the following question: *What did the* Titanic *run into?* Then, answer the question using the text you underlined to support your answer.

_____

_____

_____

_____

True/False

Directions: Write *True* or *False* next to each statement about textual evidence.

_____ **1.** Textual evidence can be used to help answer questions in reading or to provide support to a writing topic.

_____ **2.** In-text citations are required every time you write.

_____ **3.** Paraphrasing means that you write someone else's idea but you don't have to give them credit.

_____ **4.** Direct quotations are exact words used as support.

_____ **5.** An example of plagiarism would be copying two sentences that someone else wrote on the Internet and making it seem as though you were the one who wrote the words by not having an in-text citation.

Directions: Rewrite the false sentences above so that they are true statements.

_____

_____

_____

_____

_____

_____

_____

INDEPENDENT PRACTICE

Name _____   Date _____

"Should Fidget Spinners Be Banned from Schools?"

Directions: Read the passage. Then, answer the questions.

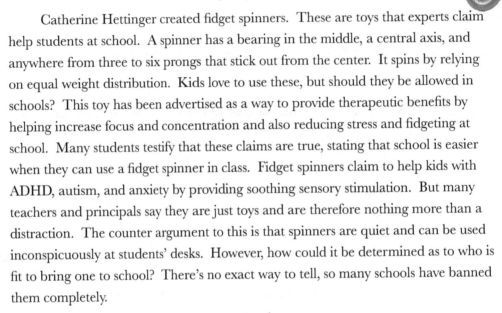

Should Fidget Spinners Be Banned from Schools?
by Jay Heller

Catherine Hettinger created fidget spinners. These are toys that experts claim help students at school. A spinner has a bearing in the middle, a central axis, and anywhere from three to six prongs that stick out from the center. It spins by relying on equal weight distribution. Kids love to use these, but should they be allowed in schools? This toy has been advertised as a way to provide therapeutic benefits by helping increase focus and concentration and also reducing stress and fidgeting at school. Many students testify that these claims are true, stating that school is easier when they can use a fidget spinner in class. Fidget spinners claim to help kids with ADHD, autism, and anxiety by providing soothing sensory stimulation. But many teachers and principals say they are just toys and are therefore nothing more than a distraction. The counter argument to this is that spinners are quiet and can be used inconspicuously at students' desks. However, how could it be determined as to who is fit to bring one to school? There's no exact way to tell, so many schools have banned them completely.

page 1

1. Highlight the textual evidence that would be best to use in a paper arguing reasons fidget spinners should be allowed in schools.

2. Underline the textual evidence that best answers the following question: *What type of kids do fidget spinners claim to help?* Then, answer the question using the text you underlined to support your answer.

_____

_____

_____

_____

_____

Tip: Text evidence should prove exactly what it is you are trying to say. They are carefully chosen words that match your question or topic exactly.

Citing with Direct Quotations

🔍 Objective

Students will find and use direct quotations and correctly cite them.

✏️ Materials

- copies of *"Namesake"* (page 22; page22.pdf)
- copies of *"A Long Lost Hero"* (page 23; page23.pdf)
- highlighters

💡 Essential Question

How do I choose a direct quotation related to a question and correctly cite it?

Guided Practice

1. Explain to students that when proving a point based on something the text says, using exact words from the text as support helps to "prove" the point. Tell students there is a way to write so the reader knows when words are from a different text.

2. Distribute *"Namesake"* (page 22). Have students take turns reading aloud. Then, ask students, *"How is Alex different from the stereotype of most other girls?"* Give students time to locate and highlight the answer.

3. Once students have located the sentence(s) that proves the answer, they must formulate their written responses. This includes accurately answering the question, providing evidence, including an in-text citation, and writing a final thought to elaborate or connect the evidence to the answer. Remind students that they must put exact text inside quotation marks. Tell students that they don't have to quote an entire sentence; they can pick only the key words that best provide the answer.

4. Remind students to use in-text citations or parenthetical references. Write several examples on the board following MLA format, such as (Button 1), (Roberts 15), (Jackson 24), (Smith par. 3), or (McDonald par. 15).

5. Have students practice with the second question, *"How do you know Jackie Mitchell was a successful baseball player?"* Guide each student in answering with a direct quotation and a citation. Redirect as needed to be sure formatting of the citation is correct. Students may choose to share their answers with the class.

Independent Practice

- Have students complete *"A Long Lost Hero"* (page 23) in class, as homework, or as an assessment to ensure they can complete the skill independently.

Additional Support

Have students annotate each individual sentence, indicating which text relates to each question.

GUIDED PRACTICE

Name _____ Date _____

"Namesake"

Directions: Answer each question using a direct quotation and an in-text citation.

Namesake
by Greg Button

My dad named me Alex, after Alex Rodriguez, the baseball player—never mind that I'm a girl. My dad always says I can do whatever I want, whether that's playing ball or playing with dolls. But I have to admit—I really do love baseball.

Want to know who my favorite player is? If you guessed A-Rod, you backed the wrong horse. It's actually Jackie Mitchell. She played for a men's AA squad—the minor leagues—when she was only 17. If that doesn't knock your socks off, maybe I ought to tell you that after Mitchell joined the Chattanooga Lookouts, they played none other than the New York Yankees.

Oh, I forgot to tell you the year was 1931! Know what that means? Babe Ruth and Lou Gehrig were on the Yankees. See where I'm going with this? This little 5'5", 130-pound missy took the mound in front of 4,000 fans. (Did I mention she was a left-handed pitcher? That's right! She was a southpaw.)

She proved good things come in small packages by delivering one, two, three strikes to Babe Ruth! Then, a really remarkable thing happened. She does the same thing with Lou Gehrig! After that, her arm starts aching, so she rests.

You can't blame Mitchell for that. The owner of the Lookouts was this crazy marketing genius who was always pulling wild stunts to attract crowds and make money. Anyway, he decided last minute to have a teenage girl play against the Yankees for the exhibition game to make it a red-letter day. So Mitchell—who was in Dallas playing in a basketball tournament—was bused back up to Tennessee. Then, she had only five days to train before playing the Yankees. Of course her arm was sore!

Unfortunately, her team ended up losing. The weird thing is that afterward, Mitchell didn't play for the Lookouts anymore. Who knows why, but she started playing for the owner's lower-level teams instead. I look at it this way: A teenage girl got paid to play men's baseball for six years. Someday, I'd like to throw like a girl, so I can be just like Jackie Mitchell. I think I could learn to strike out a Yankee or two. After all, my dad says I can do whatever I want to—even if that's playing ball in the men's league.

page 1

1. How does Alex feel about her name?

   _____

   _____

2. How do you know Jackie Mitchell was a successful baseball player?

   _____

   _____

Name _____ Date _____

"A Long Lost Hero"

Directions: Answer each question using a direct quotation and in-text citation.

A Long Lost Hero
by T. Robert Hall

Lately, my dad and I have been looking into our family's genealogy. Rooting around in our past began as a hobby for my dad, and it wasn't interesting to me. Our family tree was just a lot of boring names and dates on paper. My dad began seeking public records that revealed where our relatives lived and what they did to earn money. Then, things got kind of exciting. My dad found enlistment papers.

It turns out that we have a genuine Civil War soldier among our kin. The records say my ancestor was 18 years old when he enrolled to fight. But all these years later, my dad and I caught my ancestor in a lie. His birth record shows he was only 12!

The Confederates had assigned my cousin to the role of drummer boy. I thought drummer boys were mascots, but I found out they did a whole lot more. Some of them carried the injured away from the battlefields on stretchers. Others were messengers or orderlies. They drummed communications on the battlefield when it was too loud to hear shouts. Their drum rolls could indicate "meet here," "retreat," or even "charge."

Knowing that my rebel cousin lied about his age made him seem a lot more real. And the more I learned about him, the more I wanted to learn about our other ancestors. So now I help my dad with his hobby, which has become *our* hobby. The names and dates still aren't of much interest to me, but I keep riffling through documents in hopes of finding the next great story!

page 1

1. How did drummer boys help injured soldiers?

   _____

   _____

2. What other important way did drummers help in the war?

   _____

   _____

Tip: Be sure that you use quotation marks (" ") around the exact words used in your answer. Then, format the citation correctly—author followed by the page number. (Author __).

Citing with Block Quotations

Objective

Students will answer questions using block quotations.

Materials

- copies of *"Lost in Translation"* (page 25; page25.pdf)
- copies of *"Up Close and Personal"* (page 26; page26.pdf)
- highlighters

Essential Question

How do I properly use a block quotation?

Guided Practice

1. Explain to students that sometimes, longer excerpts can be used as strong evidence to support an answer.

2. Distribute *"Lost in Translation"* (page 25). Have students read the question, so they know what information to look for. Then, read the passage aloud. As you read, model think-aloud strategies for students. Have students annotate and highlight text that will support their answers.

3. Have students orally suggest parts of the text that directly relate to the question being asked. Explain that sometimes answers to questions will be found in the text, and sometimes they will have to be inferred. In this case, the answer comes directly from the text. However, the passage chosen to answer the question is in a longer example, therefore using a block quotation is best. Tell students that the rule of thumb is if the quotation is more than four lines of text, it should be formatted as a block quotation rather than a regular citation.

4. Explain to students that as a general pattern, questions are best answered in three parts: The first part answers the question, the second part provides text evidence as support with a text citation, and the third part elaborates or connects the evidence to the original answer.

5. Explain to students that when using a block quotation, the selection of text begins on a new line, is indented from both sides, and is followed by a citation.

Independent Practice

- Have students complete *"Up Close and Personal"* (page 26) in class, as homework, or as an assessment to ensure they can complete the skill independently.

Additional Support

Students can write the author's last name and page number in the margin next to the quotation to easily copy the in-text citation when needed.

"Lost in Translation"

Directions: Read the question at the bottom of the page. Then, read the passage. Annotate and highlight while reading to help you answer the question. Include a cited block quotation to support your answer.

Lost in Translation
by Woody Blaine

I've been fascinated by trees since as far back as I can remember. They bear the scars of all they have survived, from drought and wind to fire. And if you look and listen closely, each will tell you the story of its life. One might have witnessed the building of a beautiful trail; another will tell the tale of all the animals it has sheltered, cradling them in its arms. I find all trees mesmerizing.

The trees called me to visit Zion National Park. These trees have difficult lives, enduring high temperatures with little water to quench their thirst. They make their homes along high cliffs as they plant their roots in inhospitable rock. Yet despite the odds, twisting junipers and squat piñons, towering aspens and welcoming cottonwoods survive and even thrive.

I came to visit the trees, but it was the rocks that spoke to me. There, all along the Virgin River, hundreds of images lined the surface of the sandstone.

The sandstone faces speak not for themselves but for a people of the past. They bear messages like diaries engraved in nature, perhaps containing details about food and rain, hunting and planting, birth and death. But there is no one to interpret the messages for us. The people who left the engravings behind have long since departed this Earth.

The images might date back 1,000 years to the Ancestral Puebloan peoples. (We once called these ancient people the Anasazi, but that means "enemy ancestors" in Navajo. So now we have a more accurate name for them.) But the parklands were inhabited as far back as 7,000 years ago. There might be clues about how the ancient people lived among the petroglyphs as well.

The chiseled history contains more mysteries than answers. Here a bighorn sheep, there a herd. A humanlike figure next to a foot with six toes. A spiral, a zigzag design, and so much more. The light-colored engravings pop out against the dark desert varnish, where they've stood the test of time. They want me to hear their story, to unravel their mysteries. But I can't quite make out their whispers, which are in a language so old there is no translation. I look to the trees for answers, but they aren't talking. It isn't their tale to tell.

page 1

1. What is an example of how the author feels nature comes to life?

_____

_____

_____

Name _____ Date _____

"Up Close and Personal"

Directions: Read the question at the bottom of the page. Then, read the passage. Annotate and highlight while reading to help you answer the question. Answer the question on a separate sheet of paper, and include a cited block quotation to support your answer.

Up Close and Personal
by Charity Brinkley

"Do you have your genome map ready?" The pilot was running a final instrument check. "Fasten your seatbelt; we're about to lift off." And with that, the hover-ship darted off at such a speed that Bernadette's stomach lurched. It quickly settled when she saw the double helix coming up over the horizon as if it were a rising sun.

"Take a look at your map to get a sense of our location. We'll be starting near HERC2."

Bernadette squealed. "I know that one—it's one of the eye-color genes!" When she'd had her DNA sequence mapped, she had taken particular note of this spot. "It says on my map that my SNP is GG." She was careful to pronounce SNP as snip whenever referring to a particular DNA sequence.

The pilot smiled. "Seventy-two percent of people with GG inherit blue eyes, so your green color is a less common result. There's a neighboring gene that may have made the difference," he said, pointing toward OCA2. "Or it could be something else we haven't deciphered yet."

As they floated by sparkling strands of letters in the space-like atmosphere, Bernadette recognized another favorite SNP on the map.

"Okay," she laughed, "I know this one. I'm an AG. I can drink milk, but my mom can't. That makes the G from her and the A from my dad." It was pretty cool to see her parents' influence. She knew from her analysis that she had large pieces of DNA identical to her siblings and almost as many common portions with her cousins. She wondered how far back into her family tree she could trace those segments. She might have inherited DNA that hadn't changed in her family for generations!

Before Bernadette could get too lost in her thoughts about ancestry, the pilot directed her attention to a new location. "What's this?" she asked. It wasn't on her map.

"That's a portion of the genome we haven't decoded," he explained. "I wanted to show it to you because it will take enthusiasm like yours to uncover the mysteries human DNA still holds."

Bernadette was up to that task, but not just yet. First, she wanted to see a little bit more of that charted territory. As they piloted deeper into the double helix, Bernadette perched on the edge of her seat. There was so much to learn and explore. She didn't want to miss a thing.

page 1

1. How does Bernadette explain how her genes come from her mom and dad?

> **Tip:** Be sure your answer has three parts: answering the question, a quotation, and an in-text citation. It should end with a connection or explanation to connect your answer to the evidence used.

Citing with Paraphrasing

🔍 Objective

Students will paraphrase a text and correctly cite it.

✏️ Materials

- copies of *"Khufu's Tomb"* (page 28; page28.pdf)
- copies of *"The Dragon Jewel"* (page 29; page29.pdf)
- highlighters

💡 Essential Question

How do I find text related to a question and correctly paraphrase and cite it?

Guided Practice

1. Explain to students that sometimes exact quotations are not needed, but instead general ideas can be paraphrased. Explain that to *paraphrase* means to talk about parts of the text in one's own words. However, a citation should still be given to credit the author of the original text because it was their original thought or idea.

2. Distribute copies of *"Khufu's Tomb"* (page 28). Read the passage aloud as students follow along. After reading, ask students to think about the first question. Give students time to locate, highlight, and share examples.

3. Once students have located examples to support their answers, tell students to paraphrase the information from the text and include citations. Write an example of an MLA citation on the board: *(Williams 1)*. Guide students in formulating their responses using paraphrasing and creating the correct citations. Use the text evidence starters on pages 128–129 to aid students in choosing an appropriate starter to introduce their text evidence.

4. Have students answer the second question. Remind them that they should not have quotation marks when paraphrasing. Redirect as needed to be sure formatting of their citations is correct. Students may choose to share their answers with the class.

Independent Practice

- Have students complete *"The Dragon Jewel"* (page 29) in class, as homework, or as an assessment to ensure they can complete the skill independently.

Additional Support

Remind students of the difference between a direct quotation and paraphrasing.

Name _____   Date _____

"Khufu's Tomb"

Directions: On a separate sheet of paper, answer the questions by paraphrasing and using in-text citations.

Khufu's Tomb
by Jack Williams

Mao padded across the site, weaving in and out among the workers themselves, who were digging pits in the ground and hefting large blocks of limestone. Mao had been watching them build layer by layer here since her childhood.

The pyramid had finally taken shape now, reaching nearly 500 feet into the sky. She suspected it was the tallest in the world. Despite the frantic activity, Mao felt safe navigating the sandy grounds. She had seen men punished for harming her kind, even by accident. The workers all were cautious in her presence, both out of respect and fear of consequences. She trusted they would go out of their way to protect her.

Nearby, a worker stopped his polishing to greet her. "Ahhh, Mao. Welcome. Checking on our progress?" He nodded upward. "The core is complete, so I am preparing materials for the surface. This limestone will make Khufu's tomb shine like the sun." The white coating would contrast what Mao had seen inside. Mao could sashay herself through the small dark shafts with ease, but she had the advantage of night vision. The king's burial chamber was one of the few rooms with light. There, openings would allow Khufu to pass into the afterlife.

The king himself was visiting the site today. Mao recognized him standing over a wide pit, next to hundreds of pieces of wood. Curious, she trotted toward him. "Mao, your visit is a sign of good fortune! Today, we are preparing my boat." Mao stood by the king's side, observing workers organizing wood planks. Mao breathed in the cedar scent. The Phoenicians had crafted this ship. In their country, strong trees were plentiful.

After crossing the river Styx, Khufu would be able to sail wherever he might like. Mao circled the king's legs, and he lifted her up to his chest so she could better survey the activity. His ambitious project would bring glory to the king and to Egypt.

Contented, Mao laid her head on Khufu's shoulder as he stroked her back. She was tired from her exploration. Feeling safe in the king's arms, she shut her eyes against the bright glare of the sun and let sleep overtake her. She would dream of climbing to the top of the great white pyramid, touching the sky with the soft pads of her paws, and wandering across a pathway of stars.

page 1

1. How do you know what the secret of Mao is?

2. How can you tell Mao and the king have a close relationship?

Name _____ Date _____

"The Dragon Jewel"

INDEPENDENT PRACTICE

Directions: On a separate sheet of paper, answer the questions by paraphrasing and using in-text citations.

The Dragon Jewel (A Japanese Myth)
by Oliver Kellog

Prince Lofty declared to all that he would acquire a dragon jewel, which would require slaying the beast and taking it from his throat. Although the prince intended to acquire the jewel, you may be certain the great boaster did not propose to undertake the quest himself.

Instead, he called together a crowd of servants, gave them money for the task, and then ordered them not to show themselves again until they had brought him the jewel.

The men took the money readily enough, but not to hunt the dragon. In the meantime, Prince Lofty did not doubt he would possess the jewel and with it a princess. So he had a fine palace built, sparing no expense. The wood was inlaid with gold and precious stones, while fine painted silks hung upon the walls.

A year passed, but the men did not return. So the prince called together the servants who were left and instructed them to prepare a boat. They were frightened when they realized he intended to go after the jewel himself and shame them. "Cowards!" bellowed Prince Lofty. "Watch me and learn how to be brave. I am not afraid of the dragon, but it will fear me."

The first evening on the boat, a fierce storm brought great waves that foamed over the side as rain poured down in torrents. Brave Prince Lofty was certain they would all drown. He clung to the boat, seasick and frightened, begging the servants to save him. They told him, "My prince, the dragon sends this storm. If you promise you will not harm him, perhaps he will let us live."

Prince Lofty would promise anything to stop the storm, so he vowed never to touch the dragon, not even a hair on the tip of his tail.

The storm eventually died down, and the little boat finally reached land. When the prince at last felt the earth below his feet, he wept, proclaiming he would never leave solid ground again. Although they had landed on an island far from Japan, he would not return by boat, not for a hundred princesses. So the prince stayed there the rest of his life, and the beautiful palace he had built for the princess had no one to live in it but the bats and owls and sometimes a stray mouse or two.

page 1

1. In what ways does the prince change from the beginning to the end of the story?

2. How does Prince Lofty feel when the storm is coming?

Tip: Be sure that you use quotation marks (" ") around the exact words used in your answer. Then, format the citation correctly (Author __).

Citing with Poetry

🔍 Objective

Students will correctly use quotations and cite from poetry.

✏️ Materials

- copies of *"Fall Leaves Fall"* (page 31; page31.pdf)
- copies of *"Young and Old"* (page 32; page32.pdf)
- highlighters

💡 Essential Question

How do I properly cite lines from a poem?

Guided Practice

1. Explain to students that when using poems as text evidence, citations are treated differently from prose, or regular text. Explain that when a quotation in a poem is used and the evidence is on more than one line, a backslash is used to indicate a line break. In addition, the citation should include the author's last name and the line number(s) of the poem.

2. Distribute *"Fall Leaves Fall"* (page 31). Have students read aloud and follow along. After reading, ask students, *"How does the author feel about the transition from fall to winter?"* Give students time to locate words, phrases, or lines that might answer the question.

3. Have students orally suggest parts of the text that directly relate to the question being asked. Then, have students formulate answers to the question.

4. Guide students in developing their explanations. Remind students how to select pieces of the text that will help them develop their answers. Explain to students that even though the text might not directly state the answer, quotations can be used to support the idea that it's the best given explanation.

5. Have students complete their answers in their own words, using one or two quotations to provide support. Use the text evidence starters on pages 128–129 to aid students in choosing an appropriate starter to introduce their text evidence. Encourage students to use quotations that are more than one line long. Remind students that direct text must be quoted and cited properly. Write an example of an MLA poetry citation on the board: *"I shall sing when night's decay / Ushers in a drearier day" (Bronte 7–8).* Redirect as needed to be sure formatting of the quotation and citation are correct.

Independent Practice

- Have students complete *"Young and Old"* (page 32) in class, as homework, or as an assessment to ensure they can complete the skill independently.

Additional Support

Have students focus on quotations from single lines of poetry and simple explanations.

"Fall Leaves Fall"

GUIDED PRACTICE

Directions: Read the questions at the bottom of the page. Then, read the poem. Annotate and highlight while reading to help you answer the question. Include a cited quotation to support your answer.

Fall Leaves Fall
by Emily Bronte

Fall, leaves, fall; die, flowers, away;
Lengthen night and shorten day;
Every leaf speaks bliss to me,
Fluttering from the autumn tree.
I shall smile when wreaths of snow
Blossom where the rose should grow;
I shall sing when night's decay
Ushers in a drearier day.

1. How does the author feel about the transition from fall to winter? Explain your answer using at least two in-text citations.

_____

_____

_____

_____

_____

2. Based on the poem, which season does the author prefer?

_____

_____

_____

_____

_____

Name _____ Date _____

"Young and Old"

Directions: Read the question at the bottom of the page. Then, read the passage. Annotate and highlight while reading to help you answer the question. Include a cited quotation to support your answer.

Young and Old
by Charles Kingsley

When all the world is young, lad,
And all the trees are green;
And every goose a swan, lad,
And every lass a queen;
Then hey for boot and horse, lad,
And round the world away;
Young blood must have its course, lad,
And every dog his day.
When all the world is old, lad,
And all the trees are brown;
When all the sport is stale, lad,
And all the wheels run down;
Creep home, and take your place there,
The spent and maimed among:
God grant you find one face there,
You loved when all was young.

1. How does the author feel about getting older? Explain your answer thoroughly using at least two in-text citations.

_____

_____

_____

_____

Tip: Be sure to put a backslash between each line of text when using poetry as text evidence.

Author's Purpose

✏️ Materials

- *Author's Purpose—Annotation Example* (page 34; page34.pdf) (optional)

- copies of *Author's Purpose— "Mars Mission Application"* (pages 35–36; page35.pdf)

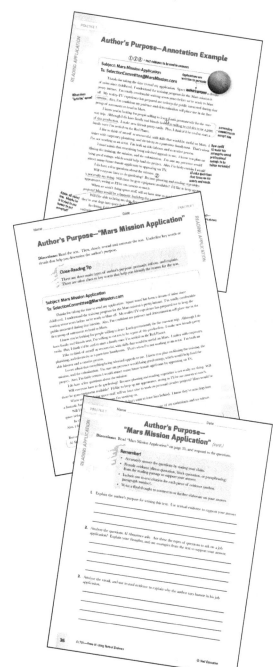

Procedure

1. Distribute *Author's Purpose—"Mars Mission Application"* (pages 35–36). Have students read the passage independently.

2. Have students reread the passage, this time completing a close reading and annotation of the text. Students should focus specifically on the close-reading skill of identifying author's purpose. Have students underline key details that help them identify the author's purpose.

   - The *Author's Purpose—Annotation Example* (page 34) can be used for your reference, to model annotating for students, or as an individual scaffold for students as necessary.

Close-Reading Skill—Identifying Author's Purpose

Explain to students that there are three main types of author's purpose: persuasive, informative, and explanatory. Tell students to look for key words that could be clues to the author's purpose. Italicized words would most likely be persuasive. Factual and organizational words are used to inform or explain, and descriptive words help with expression.

3. Assign the text-dependent questions on page 36. Explain to students that their responses should accurately answer the question, provide evidence (direct quotations, block quotations, or paraphrasing) from the reading passage to support the answers, include in-text citations, and conclude with final thoughts that connect or further explain the answers.

4. Remind students that a citation is needed directly following a quotation. In this case, the abbreviation *par.* is used to reference a specific paragraph.

Throughout this section, annotation example pages are provided for your reference. Unfortunately, due to spacing limitations, the line breaks do not match exactly to the student versions of the texts.

Author's Purpose—Annotation Example

①②③ = text evidence to be used in answers

Subject: Mars Mission Application
To: SelectionCommittee@MarsMission.com

Applications are written to persuade
↓
author's purpose

Thanks for taking the time to read my application. Space travel has been a dream of mine since childhood. I understand the training program for the Mars mission is pretty intense. I'm totally comfortable waiting seven years before we're ready to blast off. My reality-TV experience has prepared me to keep the public interested during that interim. Also, I'm confident my patience and determination will place me in the first group of astronauts to head to Mars.

What does "interim" mean?

I know you're looking for people willing to leave Earth permanently for the one-way trip. Although I do have family and friends here, ① I'm willing to cut ties to be a part of this production. I make new friends pretty easily. Plus, I think it'd be cool to start a family once I'm settled on the Red Planet.

persuading committee to accept him

I like to think of myself as resourceful, with skills that would be useful on Mars. I tinker with carpentry, plumbing, and electricity as a part-time handyman. That's when I'm not working as an actor. I'm both an able laborer and a creative person.

How could Al make his strengths sound professional enough to be taken seriously?

I must admit that everything being televised appeals to me. I know you plan on filming the training, the mission, and the colonization. I'm sure my presence would bring good ratings, which would help fund the project. Also, I'm fairly certain I would attract many future female applicants by appearing on TV.

Al asks questions that focus on his wants and needs.

I do have a few questions about the mission: ②

Will everyone have to do gardening? Because planting and tending vegetables is not really my thing. Will there be gym equipment available? I'd like to keep up my appearance, seeing as I'll be on camera so much.

When we aren't doing space stuff, will we have time to work on personal creative projects? Mars would be a fantastic backdrop for a sci-fi feature I'm working on.

Again, all about him. Maybe he is trying to use humor to get accepted?

Will I be able to bring my dog, Rover? I don't want to leave him behind. I know they've sent dogs into space before. ③ Also, animals have high audience appeal.

He has a point—everyone loves shows with animals!

In closing, I think you should include me in your program because of my enthusiasm and my talents. Also, I think you'll find I'm a true representative of Earth today.

Thank you for your consideration.

Best regards,
Al Aboutmee

Author's Purpose—"Mars Mission Application"

Directions: Read the text. Then, closely reread and annotate the text. Underline key words or details that help you determine the author's purpose.

> ### Close-Reading Tip
>
> There are three main types of author's purpose: persuade, inform, and explain. There are often clues or key words that help you identify the reason for the text.

Subject: Mars Mission Application
To: SelectionCommittee@MarsMission.com

Thanks for taking the time to read my application. Space travel has been a dream of mine since childhood. I understand the training program for the Mars mission is pretty intense. I'm totally comfortable waiting seven years before we're ready to blast off. My reality-TV experience has prepared me to keep the public interested during that interim. Also, I'm confident my patience and determination will place me in the first group of astronauts to head to Mars.

I know you're looking for people willing to leave Earth permanently for the one-way trip. Although I do have family and friends here, I'm willing to cut ties to be a part of this production. I make new friends pretty easily. Plus, I think it'd be cool to start a family once I'm settled on the Red Planet.

I like to think of myself as resourceful, with skills that would be useful on Mars. I tinker with carpentry, plumbing, and electricity as a part-time handyman. That's when I'm not working as an actor. I'm both an able laborer and a creative person.

I must admit that everything being televised appeals to me. I know you plan on filming the training, the mission, and the colonization. I'm sure my presence would bring good ratings, which would help fund the project. Also, I'm fairly certain I would attract many future female applicants by appearing on TV.

I do have a few questions about the mission:

Will everyone have to do gardening? Because planting and tending vegetables is not really my thing. Will there be gym equipment available? I'd like to keep up my appearance, seeing as I'll be on camera so much.

When we aren't doing space stuff, will we have time to work on personal creative projects? Mars would be a fantastic backdrop for a sci-fi feature I'm working on.

Will I be able to bring my dog, Rover? I don't want to leave him behind. I know they've sent dogs into space before. Also, animals have high audience appeal.

In closing, I think you should include me in your program because of my enthusiasm and my talents. Also, I think you'll find I'm a true representative of Earth today.

Thank you for your consideration.

Best regards,

Al Aboutmee

Author's Purpose—
"Mars Mission Application" *(cont.)*

Directions: Read "Mars Mission Application" on page 35, and respond to the questions.

> ### Remember!
> - Accurately answer the questions by stating your claim.
> - Provide evidence (direct quotation, block quotation, or paraphrasing) from the reading passage to support your answer.
> - Include one in-text citation for each piece of evidence (author, paragraph number).
> - Write a final thought to connect to or further elaborate on your answer.

1. Explain the author's purpose for writing this text. Use textual evidence to support your answer.

   _____

   _____

   _____

2. Analyze the questions Al Aboutmee asks. Are these the types of questions to ask on a job application? Explain your thoughts, and use examples from the text to support your answer.

   _____

   _____

   _____

   _____

3. Analyze the email, and use textual evidence to explain why the author uses humor in his job application.

   _____

   _____

   _____

   _____

Text Structure

✏️ Materials

- *Text Structure—Annotation Example* (page 38; page38.pdf) (optional)

- copies of *Text Structure— "DIY: Homemade Fireworks"* (pages 39–40; page39.pdf)

Procedure

1. Distribute *Text Structure—"DIY: Homemade Fireworks"* (pages 39–40), and have students read the passage independently.

2. Have students skim the passage first, looking for signal words that help identify how the text is organized. Then, have students put boxes around the key words that help identify structure.

   - The *Text Structure—Annotation Example* (page 38) can be used for your reference, to model annotating for students, or as an individual scaffold for students as necessary.

Close-Reading Skill—Identifying Text Structure

Explain to students that text structure is how the information is organized. Text structure includes the following frameworks: *compare and contrast, description, problem and solution, chronological or sequence, cause and effect,* and *directions.*

3. Assign the text-dependent questions on the activity page. Students should accurately answer the questions, provide evidence (direct quotation or paraphrasing) from the reading passage to support their answers, include in-text citations, and write final thoughts to connect or further explain their answers.

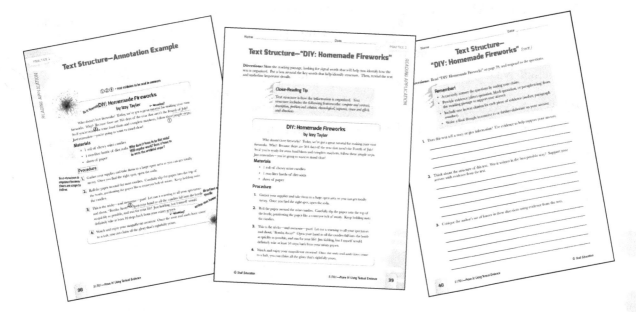

Text Structure—Annotation Example

①②③ = text evidence to be used in answers

Do It Yourself DIY: Homemade Fireworks
by Izzy Tayler

v- meaning?

Who doesn't love fireworks? Today, we've got a great <u>tutorial</u> for making your own fireworks. Why? Because there are 364 days of the year that aren't the Fourth of July! So if you're ready ③ for some loud blasts and complete mayhem, follow these simple steps. ① Just remember—you're going to want to stand clear!

Materials

- 1 roll of chewy mint candies
- 1 two-liter bottle of diet soda
- sheet of paper

Why does it have to be diet soda? Will regular work? Does it have to do with the artificial sugar?

Procedure

Text structure is sequence because there are steps to follow.

1. Gather your supplies and take them to a large open area so you can get totally messy. Once you find the right spot, open the soda.

2. Roll the paper around the mint candies. Carefully slip the paper into the top of the bottle, positioning the paper like a conveyor belt of mints. Keep holding onto the candies.

3. This is the tricky—and awesome—part! Let out a warning to all your spectators and shout, "Bombs Away!" ② Open your hand so all the candies fall into the bottle as quickly as possible, and run for your life! Just kidding, but I myself would definitely take at least 10 steps back from your minty geyser.

directions are specific

author uses humor

v- meaning?

4. Watch and enjoy your magnificent creation! Once the *ooohs* and *aaahs* have come to a halt, you can claim all the glory that's rightfully yours.

51701—Prove It! Using Textual Evidence

Name _____ Date _____

Text Structure—"DIY: Homemade Fireworks"

Directions: Skim the reading passage, looking for signal words that will help you identify how the text is organized. Put a box around the key words that help identify structure. Then, reread the text and underline important details.

Close-Reading Tip

Text structure is how the information is organized. Text structure includes the following frameworks: *compare and contrast, description, problem and solution, chronological, sequence, cause and effect,* and *directions.*

DIY: Homemade Fireworks
by Izzy Tayler

Who doesn't love fireworks? Today, we've got a great tutorial for making your own fireworks. Why? Because there are 364 days of the year that aren't the Fourth of July! So if you're ready for some loud blasts and complete mayhem, follow these simple steps. Just remember—you're going to want to stand clear!

Materials

- 1 roll of chewy mint candies
- 1 two-liter bottle of diet soda
- sheet of paper

Procedure

1. Gather your supplies and take them to a large open area so you can get totally messy. Once you find the right spot, open the soda.

2. Roll the paper around the mint candies. Carefully slip the paper into the top of the bottle, positioning the paper like a conveyor belt of mints. Keep holding onto the candies.

3. This is the tricky—and awesome—part! Let out a warning to all your spectators and shout, "Bombs Away!" Open your hand so all the candies fall into the bottle as quickly as possible, and run for your life! Just kidding, but I myself would definitely take at least 10 steps back from your minty geyser.

4. Watch and enjoy your magnificent creation! Once the *ooohs* and *aaahs* have come to a halt, you can claim all the glory that's rightfully yours.

Text Structure—
"DIY: Homemade Fireworks" *(cont.)*

Directions: Read "DIY: Homemade Fireworks" on page 39, and respond to the questions.

> ### Remember!
> - Accurately answer the questions by stating your claim.
> - Provide evidence (direct quotation, block quotation, or paraphrasing) from the reading passage to support your answer.
> - Include one in-text citation for each piece of evidence (author, paragraph number).
> - Write a final thought to connect to or further elaborate on your answer.

1. Does this text tell a story or give information? Use evidence to help support your answer.

   _____

   _____

   _____

2. Think about the structure of this text. Was it written in the best possible way? Support your answer with evidence from the text.

   _____

   _____

   _____

   _____

3. Critique the author's use of humor in these directions using evidence from the text.

   _____

   _____

   _____

   _____

Main Idea

✏️ Materials

- *Main Idea—Annotation Example* (page 42; page42.pdf) (optional)

- copies of *Main Idea—Excerpt from "Dr. Martin Luther King Jr."* (pages 43–44; page43.pdf)

Procedure

1. Distribute copies of *Main Idea—Excerpt from "Dr. Martin Luther King Jr."* (pages 43–44). Have students read the passage independently.

2. Have students reread and complete a close reading and annotation of the text. Students should focus on the close-reading skill of determining the main idea. Have students underline the main idea in each paragraph.

   - The *Main Idea—Annotation Example* (page 42) can be used for your reference, to model annotating for students, or as an individual scaffold for students as necessary.

3. Tell students to use the underlined details to identify the main idea of each paragraph. Then, have them write the main idea in the margins next to the paragraphs.

> **Close-Reading Skill—Determining Main Idea**
>
> Explain to students that the main idea is the overall idea of a text. It is sometimes easily found, and other times it is more difficult. Tell students that identifying main details will help determine the main idea of a text.

4. Assign the text-dependent questions on page 44. Explain to students that their responses should accurately answer the question, provide evidence (direct quotations, block quotations, or paraphrasing) from the reading passage to support the answers, include in-text citations, and conclude with final thoughts that connect or further explain the answers.

5. Remind students that a citation is needed directly following a quotation. In this case, the abbreviation *par.* is used to reference a specific paragraph.

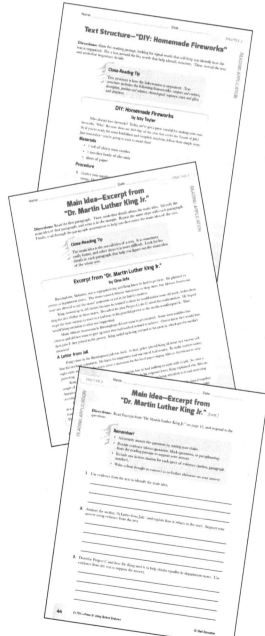

READING APPLICATION

Main Idea—Annotation Example

①②③ = text evidence to be used in answers

M.I. = Main Idea

Excerpt from "Dr. Martin Luther King Jr."

by Gina Jefe

v- meaning?

Birmingham, Alabama, was a segregated city, and King knew he had to go there. **M.I. locations of protest**

Interesting that King wanted to act in a peaceful manner to get the storeowners to become angry.

He planned to protest at department stores. The stores wanted African Americans to shop there, but African Americans were not allowed to use the stores' restrooms or eat at the lunch counters. ③

King showed up in old clothes because he wanted to show he would rather wear **M.I. Project C** old work clothes than shop for nice clothes at these stores. He called the plan Project C; the C stood for confrontation. He hoped to get the store owners to react in a bad way to his peaceful protest so the media would report it. That would bring attention to what was happening.

Many African Americans in Birmingham did not want to get involved. Some **M.I. African Americans reluctant to get involved** were middle-class citizens and did not want to give up what they had worked so hard to achieve. Others knew they would lose their jobs if they joined in the protest. King ended up being arrested at the protest, which got the media's attention!

A Letter from Jail

Even though he was locked up, King accomplished what he wanted—the media's attention.

King's time in the Birmingham jail was hard. At first, police placed King all alone in a narrow cell that did not have a mattress. He knew his supporters had run out of **M.I. difficult time in jail** bail money. To make matters worse, eight white ministers in the town wrote a statement for the local paper urging African Americans to stop protesting.

King felt that he must respond to this statement, but he had nothing to write **M.I. response letter** with in jail. So, over a couple of days, his lawyer smuggled in a pen and paper. In his ② response letter, King explained why African Americans had to protest. He said the only way to spur change was to bring attention to it and protesting accomplishes this. Only then will people see that change is necessary.

What could have been the outcome if King did not use civil disobedience?

His arrest got the attention King wanted. More than 1,000 children and young adults joined together at a church and held a peaceful meeting. Unfortunately, the **M.I. King succeeded w/ peaceful protest** police brought in dogs to attack them and fire hoses to spray them. The media caught this on tape, and the nation watched these terrible events in horror. Through peaceful actions, King got the nation's attention focused on the civil rights problem. ①

Main Idea—Excerpt from "Dr. Martin Luther King Jr."

Directions: Read the first paragraph. Then, underline details about the main idea. Identify the main idea of that paragraph, and write it in the margin. Repeat the same steps with each paragraph. Finally, read through the paragraph annotations to help you determine the main idea of the text.

Close-Reading Tip

The main idea is the overall idea of a text. It is sometimes easily found, and other times it is more difficult. Look for key details in each paragraph that help you figure out the main idea of the whole text.

Excerpt from "Dr. Martin Luther King Jr."
by Gina Jefe

Birmingham, Alabama, was a segregated city, and King knew he had to go there. He planned to protest at department stores. The stores wanted African Americans to shop there, but African Americans were not allowed to use the stores' restrooms or eat at the lunch counters.

King showed up in old clothes because he wanted to show he would rather wear old work clothes than shop for nice clothes at these stores. He called the plan Project C; the C stood for confrontation. He hoped to get the store owners to react in a bad way to his peaceful protest so the media would report it. That would bring attention to what was happening.

Many African Americans in Birmingham did not want to get involved. Some were middle-class citizens and did not want to give up what they had worked so hard to achieve. Others knew they would lose their jobs if they joined in the protest. King ended up being arrested at the protest, which got the media's attention!

A Letter from Jail

King's time in the Birmingham jail was hard. At first, police placed King all alone in a narrow cell that did not have a mattress. He knew his supporters had run out of bail money. To make matters worse, eight white ministers in the town wrote a statement for the local paper urging African Americans to stop protesting.

King felt that he must respond to this statement, but he had nothing to write with in jail. So, over a couple of days, his lawyer smuggled in a pen and paper. In his response letter, King explained why African Americans had to protest. He said the only way to spur change was to bring attention to it and protesting accomplishes this. Only then will people see that change is necessary.

His arrest got the attention King wanted. More than 1,000 children and young adults joined together at a church and held a peaceful meeting. Unfortunately, the police brought in dogs to attack them and fire hoses to spray them. The media caught this on tape, and the nation watched these terrible events in horror. Through peaceful actions, King got the nation's attention focused on the civil rights problem.

Main Idea—Excerpt from "Dr. Martin Luther King Jr." *(cont.)*

Directions: Read Excerpt from "Dr. Martin Luther King Jr." on page 43, and respond to the questions.

Remember!
- Accurately answer the questions by stating your claim.
- Provide evidence (direct quotation, block quotation, or paraphrasing) from the reading passage to support your answer.
- Include one in-text citation for each piece of evidence (author, paragraph number).
- Write a final thought to connect to or further elaborate on your answer.

1. Use evidence from the text to identify the main idea.

   _____

   _____

   _____

2. Analyze the section, "A Letter from Jail," and explain how it relates to the story. Support your answer using evidence from the text.

   _____

   _____

   _____

   _____

3. Describe Project C and how Dr. King used it to help obtain equality in department stores. Use evidence from the text to support the answer.

   _____

   _____

   _____

   _____

Identifying Literary Devices

🖊 Materials

- *Identifying Literary Devices— Annotation Example* (page 46; page46.pdf) (optional)
- copies of *Identifying Literary Devices—"Race the Wind"* (pages 47–48; page47.pdf)

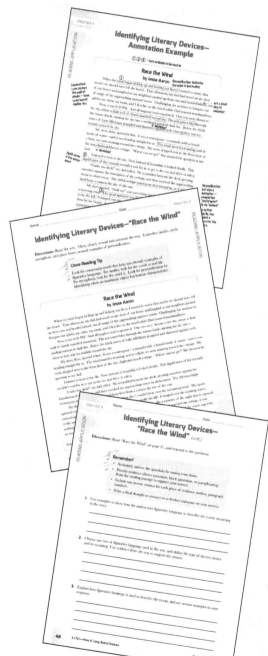

Procedure

1. Distribute copies of *Identifying Literary Devices—"Race the Wind"* (pages 47–48), and have students read the passage independently.

2. Have students reread and complete a close reading and annotation of the text. Students should underline similes, circle metaphors, and place boxes around personification.

   - The *Identifying Literary Devices—Annotation Example* (page 46) can be used for your reference, to model annotating for students, or as an individual scaffold for students as necessary.

Close-Reading Focus—Identifying Literary Devices in Texts

Metaphors and similes are two of the most commonly used types of figurative language. Tell students to look for connecting words that help identify figurative language. For similes, students should look for the words *as* and *like*. For metaphors, students should look for the word *is*. Personification is giving human characteristics to an object or something from nature. For example, *The sun peeked through the trees*.

3. Assign the text-dependent questions on page 48. Explain to students that their responses should accurately answer the question, provide evidence (direct quotations, block quotations, or paraphrasing) from the reading passage to support the answers, include in-text citations, and conclude with final thoughts that connect or further explain the answers.

4. Remind students that a citation is needed directly following a quotation. In this case, the abbreviation *par.* is used to reference a specific paragraph.

Identifying Literary Devices—
Annotation Example

① ② ③ = text evidence to be used in answers

Race the Wind
by Jesse Aaron

Personification, indicates the wind is increasing

①
When the sand began kicking up and lashing our faces, I started to worry that maybe we should have left the beach. That afternoon, my dad had stood on the deck of our home and laughed as our neighbors packed up their cars and headed inland, out *not a good idea to endanger family* of range of the approaching summer storm. Challenging the weather to dampen our spirits, my sister, my mom, and I lit a fire on the beach while Dad roasted marshmallows.

Connection: I can picture the wall of clouds— have experienced similar sky

Now, it was 6:30 PM. And all laughter had evaporated. Our eyes were drawn to the sky, where a dark wall of clouds marched toward us. The red sunset bled through the storm clouds, turning the sky into a swirling torrent of dark fire. Below, the black *v- meaning?* waves of Lake Michigan grappled and slammed against each other as they sent icy tendrils toward the sky.

My sister, Kim, spotted it first. It was a waterspout—a tornado with a funnel made of water—and it was heading straight for us. The wind started screaming, and in a flash, we were running toward the cottage. My mom stopped next to the front door of the tiny clapboard beach cottage. "Where can we go?" She shouted the question at my dad. *v- meaning?*

③
liquid sister is the water spout
I turned to look at the sky. Now, instead of beautiful, it looked deadly. This liquid sister of the tornado wouldn't wait for us to get in the car and drive to safety.

"Under the deck!" my dad yelled. We scrambled beneath the deck, pressing ourselves against the foundation of the cottage, and then watched the approaching storm in silent terror. The 200-foot-high waterspout shot toward us, as if it had been fired from a cannon the size of the sun.

Personification, but also a metephor— comparing "waterspout" to an "animal"

My dad shouted, "Hold on!" and something else I couldn't hear over the screaming wind. ② The spout sprinted over the final stretch of water, an animal eager to make the kill. It lunged over the crashing waves, twisted through the blood-red sky, and then hit the beach. And then, like a monster of the night that is exposed to the sun, the *The author using fig. lan. to paint a picture for the readers.* waterspout began to disintegrate when it hit land. By the time it reached our cottage, it was nothing more than a strong gust of water-colored wind that pelted our bodies. The rest of the storm raged for an hour and then simply blew away.

"Next time, we'll stay inland at Grandma's. Okay?" my dad said, tears of relief in his eyes. We all agreed that would be a good idea.

This could have been avoided if the family would have gone to Grandma's in the first place.

51701—Prove It! Using Textual Evidence © Shell Education

Identifying Literary Devices—"Race the Wind"

Directions: Read the text. Then, closely reread and annotate the text. Underline similes, circle metaphors, and place boxes around examples of personification.

Close-Reading Tip

Look for connecting words that help you identify examples of figurative language. For similes, look for the words *as* and *like*. For metaphors, look for the word *is*. Look for personification by identifying when an inanimate object has human characteristics.

Race the Wind
by Jesse Aaron

When the sand began kicking up and lashing our faces, I started to worry that maybe we should have left the beach. That afternoon, my dad had stood on the deck of our home and laughed as our neighbors packed up their cars and headed inland, out of range of the approaching summer storm. Challenging the weather to dampen our spirits, my sister, my mom, and I lit a fire on the beach while Dad roasted marshmallows.

Now, it was 6:30 PM. And all laughter had evaporated. Our eyes were drawn to the sky, where a dark wall of clouds marched toward us. The red sunset bled through the storm clouds, turning the sky into a swirling torrent of dark fire. Below, the black waves of Lake Michigan grappled and slammed against each other as they sent icy tendrils toward the sky.

My sister, Kim, spotted it first. It was a waterspout—a tornado with a funnel made of water—and it was heading straight for us. The wind started screaming, and in a flash, we were running toward the cottage. My mom stopped next to the front door of the tiny clapboard beach cottage. "Where can we go?" She shouted the question at my dad.

I turned to look at the sky. Now, instead of beautiful, it looked deadly. This liquid sister of the tornado wouldn't wait for us to get in the car and drive to safety.

"Under the deck!" my dad yelled. We scrambled beneath the deck, pressing ourselves against the foundation of the cottage, and then watched the approaching storm in silent terror. The 200-foot-high waterspout shot toward us, as if it had been fired from a cannon the size of the sun.

My dad shouted, "Hold on!" and something else I couldn't hear over the screaming wind. The spout sprinted over the final stretch of water, an animal eager to make the kill. It lunged over the crashing waves, twisted through the blood-red sky, and then hit the beach. And then, like a monster of the night that is exposed to the sun, the waterspout began to disintegrate when it hit land. By the time it reached our cottage, it was nothing more than a strong gust of water-colored wind that pelted our bodies. The rest of the storm raged for an hour and then simply blew away.

"Next time, we'll stay inland at Grandma's. Okay?" my dad said, tears of relief in his eyes. We all agreed that would be a good idea.

Name _____ Date _____

Identifying Literary Devices— "Race the Wind" *(cont.)*

Directions: Read "Race the Wind" on page 47, and respond to the questions.

> **Remember!**
> - Accurately answer the questions by stating your claim.
> - Provide evidence (direct quotation, block quotation, or paraphrasing) from the reading passage to support your answer.
> - Include one in-text citation for each piece of evidence (author, paragraph number).
> - Write a final thought to connect to or further elaborate on your answer.

1. Use examples to show how the author uses figurative language to describe the events occurring in the story.

   _____

   _____

   _____

2. Choose one line of figurative language used in the text, and define the type of literary device and its meaning. Use evidence from the text to support the answer.

   _____

   _____

   _____

   _____

3. Explain how figurative language is used to describe the storm, and use several examples in your response.

   _____

   _____

   _____

   _____

51701—Prove It! Using Textual Evidence   © *Shell Education*

Compare and Contrast

Materials

- *Compare and Contrast—Annotation Example* (page 50; page50.pdf) (optional)

- copies of *Compare and Contrast—"The Golden Age—from Old Greek Stories"* (pages 51–52; page51.pdf)

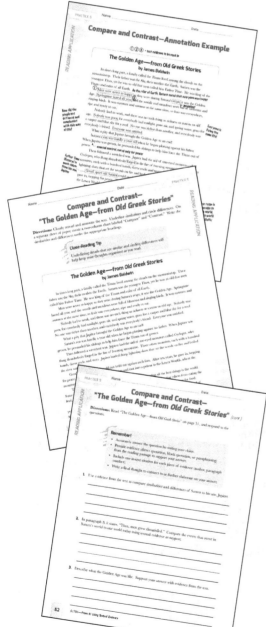

Procedure

1. Distribute copies of *Compare and Contrast—"The Golden Age—from Old Greek Stories"* (pages 51–52). Remind students that as they read, they should be focusing on the close-reading skill of identifying similarities and differences.

2. Have students closely read the passage, underlining similarities and circling differences.

   - The *Compare and Contrast—Annotation Example* (page 50) can be used for your reference, to model annotating for students, or as an individual scaffold for students as necessary.

3. On separate paper, have students create two-column charts labeled "Compare" and "Contrast." Have students write the information they underlined or circled under the appropriate headings. This will make it easier to identify information to use in their answers.

> ### Close-Reading Skill—Compare and Contrast
>
> Explain to students that comparing and contrasting is finding the similarities and differences between two or more texts. Using underlines and circles will help keep their thoughts organized.

4. Assign the text-dependent questions on page 52. Students should accurately answer the question, provide evidence (direct quotation, block quotations, or paraphrasing) from the reading passage to support their answers, include in-text citations, and conclude with final thoughts that connect or further explain their answers.

5. Remind students that a citation is needed directly following a quotation. In this case, the abbreviation *par.* is used to reference a specific paragraph.

Compare and Contrast—Annotation Example

①②③ = text evidence to be used in answers

The Golden Age—from Old Greek Stories
by James Baldwin

In times long past, a family called the Titans lived among the clouds on the mountaintop. Their father was the Sky, their mother the Earth. Saturn was the youngest Titan, yet he was so old that men called him Father Time. He was king of the Titans and ruler of all Earth. *As the ruler of Earth, Saturn cared that everyone was happy*

① Men were never so happy as they were during Saturn's reign; it was the Golden ③ Age. Springtime lasted all year, and the woods and meadows were full of blossoms and singing birds. It was summer and autumn at the same time, so fruit was everywhere, ripe and ready to eat.

v- meaning?

Nobody had to work, and there was no such thing as sickness or sorrow or old age. Nobody was poor, for everybody had sunlight, pure air, and spring water, grass for a carpet and blue sky for a roof. No one was richer than another, and everybody was everybody's friend. Everyone was satisfied.

Everyone is living the same life!

How did the people not get bored and complacent with this way of life?

What a pity that Jupiter brought the Golden Age to an end!

Saturn's son was hardly a year old when he began plotting against his father. When Jupiter was grown, he persuaded his siblings to help him force the Titans out of power. *— wanted control, cared only for power*

Then followed a wretched war. Jupiter had the aid of one-eyed monsters called Cyclops, who flung thunderbolts forged in the fire of burning mountains. Three other monsters, each with a hundred hands, threw rocks and trees. Jupiter hurled sharp lightning darts that set the woods on fire and boiled the river water.

Father Time (Saturn) is much older than his son, Jupiter

Good, quiet old Saturn could not hold out against such foes. After ten years, he gave in, begging for peace. The Titans were bound in chains and cast into a prison in the Lower Worlds, where the monsters became their jailers. ②

① Then, men grew dissatisfied. Some wanted to be rich, owning all the best things in the world. Some wanted to be kings, controlling others. Some cut down trees, preventing others from eating the fruit. Some hunted timid animals that had been their friends, killing the poor creatures for food.

v- meaning?

Jupiter reign is comparable to today's world, Saturn's world is unrealistic; fantasy

Instead of everybody being everybody's friend, everybody was everybody's enemy. Instead of peace, there was war; instead of plenty, there was starvation; instead of innocence, there was crime; and instead of joy, there was misery.

The new world was the exact opposite of the old one.

That was the way Jupiter made himself so mighty, and that was the way the Golden Age came to an end.

Compare and Contrast—
"The Golden Age—from *Old Greek Stories*"

Directions: Closely reread and annotate the text. Underline similarities and circle differences. On a separate sheet of paper, create a two-column chart labeled "Compare" and "Contrast." Write the similarities and differences under the appropriate headings.

Close-Reading Tip

Underlining details that are similar and circling differences will help keep your thoughts organized as you read.

The Golden Age—from *Old Greek Stories*
by James Baldwin

In times long past, a family called the Titans lived among the clouds on the mountaintop. Their father was the Sky, their mother the Earth. Saturn was the youngest Titan, yet he was so old that men called him Father Time. He was king of the Titans and ruler of all Earth.

Men were never so happy as they were during Saturn's reign; it was the Golden Age. Springtime lasted all year, and the woods and meadows were full of blossoms and singing birds. It was summer and autumn at the same time, so fruit was everywhere, ripe and ready to eat.

Nobody had to work, and there was no such thing as sickness or sorrow or old age. Nobody was poor, for everybody had sunlight, pure air, and spring water, grass for a carpet and blue sky for a roof. No one was richer than another, and everybody was everybody's friend. Everyone was satisfied.

What a pity that Jupiter brought the Golden Age to an end!

Saturn's son was hardly a year old when he began plotting against his father. When Jupiter was grown, he persuaded his siblings to help him force the Titans out of power.

Then followed a wretched war. Jupiter had the aid of one-eyed monsters called Cyclops, who flung thunderbolts forged in the fire of burning mountains. Three other monsters, each with a hundred hands, threw rocks and trees. Jupiter hurled sharp lightning darts that set the woods on fire and boiled the river water.

Good, quiet old Saturn could not hold out against such foes. After ten years, he gave in, begging for peace. The Titans were bound in chains and cast into a prison in the Lower Worlds, where the monsters became their jailers.

Then, men grew dissatisfied. Some wanted to be rich, owning all the best things in the world. Some wanted to be kings, controlling others. Some cut down trees, preventing others from eating the fruit. Some hunted timid animals that had been their friends, killing the poor creatures for food.

Instead of everybody being everybody's friend, everybody was everybody's enemy. Instead of peace, there was war; instead of plenty, there was starvation; instead of innocence, there was crime; and instead of joy, there was misery.

That was the way Jupiter made himself so mighty, and that was the way the Golden Age came to an end.

Compare and Contrast—
"The Golden Age—from *Old Greek Stories*" *(cont.)*

Directions: Read "The Golden Age—from *Old Greek Stories*" on page 51, and respond to the questions.

Remember!

- Accurately answer the question by stating your claim.
- Provide evidence (direct quotation, block quotation, or paraphrasing) from the reading passage to support your answer.
- Include one in-text citation for each piece of evidence (author, paragraph number).
- Write a final thought to connect to or further elaborate on your answer.

1. Use evidence from the text to compare similarities and differences of Saturn to his son, Jupiter.

_____

_____

_____

_____

2. In paragraph 8, it states, "Then, men grew dissatisfied." Compare the events that occur in Saturn's world to our world today using textual evidence as support.

_____

_____

_____

3. Describe what the Golden Age was like. Support your answer with evidence from the text.

_____

_____

_____

_____

Synthesizing and Summarizing

Materials

- *Synthesizing and Summarizing—Annotation Example* (page 54; page54.pdf) (optional)

- copies of *Synthesizing and Summarizing—Excerpt from "The Bread Book"* (pages 55–56; page55.pdf)

Procedure

1. Distribute *Synthesizing and Summarizing—Excerpt from "The Bread Book"* (pages 55–56). Have students read the passage independently.

2. Have students read the questions first. Then, have students reread the text and write an "I" next to interesting information or an "S" next to what's important.

   - The *Synthesizing and Summarizing—Annotation Example* (page 54) can be used for your reference, to model annotating for students, or as an individual scaffold for students as necessary.

Close-Reading Skill—Synthesizing and Summarizing

Explain to students that synthesizing during reading means to separate important information from interesting information. This helps when summarizing a text. Remind students that summarizing is retelling in a brief statement.

3. Assign the text-dependent questions on page 56. Students should accurately answer the question, provide evidence (direct quotation, block quotations, or paraphrasing) from the reading passage to support their answers, include in-text citations, and write final thoughts to connect or further explain their answers.

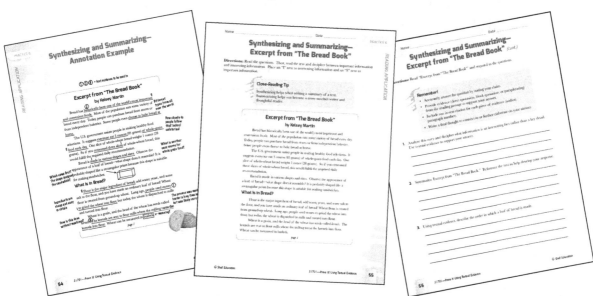

Synthesizing and Summarizing— Annotation Example

① ② ③ = text evidence to be used in answers

Excerpt from "The Bread Book"
by Kelsey Martin

②
Bread has historically been one of the world's most important **S**
and convenient foods. Most of the population eats some variety of *Different types from all over the world*
bread every day. Today, people can purchase bread from stores or
from independent bakeries. Some people even choose to bake bread at
home.

The U.S. government assists people in making healthy food *How closely do people follow this? (school cafeterias)*
selections. It suggests everyone eat 3 ounces (85 grams) of whole-grain
S food each day. One slice of whole-wheat bread weighs 1 ounce (28
grams). So if you consumed three slices of whole-wheat bread, this
would fulfill the required daily recommendation.

What is another easy source for whole grain food?

Bread is made in various shapes and sizes. Observe the
Which came first? The shape designed the sandwhich? appearance of a loaf of bread—what shape does it resemble? It is
probably shaped like a rectangular prism because this shape is suitable
for making sandwiches.

What Is in Bread?

S Flour is the major ingredient of bread; add water, yeast, and some
Ingredients are cheap and easy to obtain salt to the flour, and you have made an ordinary loaf of bread! Wheat
flour is created from ground-up wheat. Long ago, people used stones ①
to grind the wheat into flour, but today, the wheat is dispatched to mills
and turned into flour.

How is this done without machines? Wheat is a grain, and the head of the wheat has seeds called
The process was much harder a long time ago, but was likely very filling
kernels. ③ The kernels are sent to flour mills where the milling turns the
kernels into flour. Wheat can be measured in bushels. *v- meaning?*

page 1

Synthesizing and Summarizing— Excerpt from "The Bread Book"

Directions: Read the questions. Then, read the text and decipher between important information and interesting information. Place an "I" next to interesting information and an "S" next to important information.

> ### Close-Reading Tip
>
> Synthesizing helps when writing a summary of a text. Summarizing helps you become a more succinct writer and thoughtful reader.

Excerpt from "The Bread Book"
by Kelsey Martin

Bread has historically been one of the world's most important and convenient foods. Most of the population eats some variety of bread every day. Today, people can purchase bread from stores or from independent bakeries. Some people even choose to bake bread at home.

The U.S. government assists people in making healthy food selections. It suggests everyone eat 3 ounces (85 grams) of whole-grain food each day. One slice of whole-wheat bread weighs 1 ounce (28 grams). So if you consumed three slices of whole-wheat bread, this would fulfill the required daily recommendation.

Bread is made in various shapes and sizes. Observe the appearance of a loaf of bread—what shape does it resemble? It is probably shaped like a rectangular prism because this shape is suitable for making sandwiches.

What Is in Bread?

Flour is the major ingredient of bread; add water, yeast, and some salt to the flour, and you have made an ordinary loaf of bread! Wheat flour is created from ground-up wheat. Long ago, people used stones to grind the wheat into flour, but today, the wheat is dispatched to mills and turned into flour.

Wheat is a grain, and the head of the wheat has seeds called *kernels*. The kernels are sent to flour mills where the milling turns the kernels into flour. Wheat can be measured in bushels.

page 1

READING APPLICATION

Synthesizing and Summarizing— Excerpt from "The Bread Book" *(cont.)*

Directions: Read "Excerpt from 'The Bread Book'" and respond to the questions.

> ## Remember!
> - Accurately answer the question by stating your claim.
> - Provide evidence (direct quotation, block quotation, or paraphrasing) from the reading passage to support your answer.
> - Include one in-text citation for each piece of evidence (author, paragraph number).
> - Write a final thought to connect to or further elaborate on your answer.

1. Analyze this story and decipher what information is an interesting fact rather than a key detail. Use textual evidence to support your answer.

   _____

   _____

   _____

2. Summarize Excerpt from "The Bread Book." Reference the text to help develop your response.

   _____

   _____

   _____

   _____

3. Using textual evidence, describe the order in which a loaf of bread is made.

   _____

   _____

   _____

   _____

Making Inferences

✏️ Materials

- *Making Inferences—Annotation Example* (page 58; page58.pdf) (optional)
- copies of *Making Inferences— "Waiting and Watching"* (pages 59-60; page59.pdf)

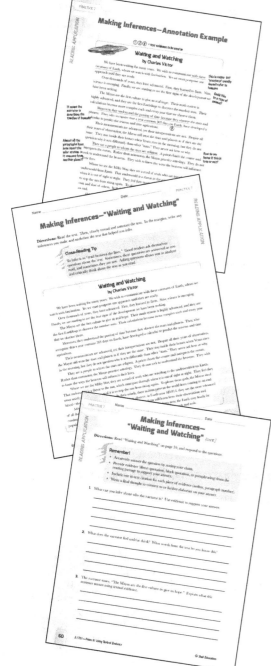

Procedure

1. Distribute copies of *Making Inferences—"Waiting and Watching"* (page 59). Have students read the passage independently.

2. Have students reread and complete a close reading and annotation of the text. Students should focus on the close-reading skill of making inferences by annotating any in the margins. Have students write in the margins what inferences they make and underline the text that led them to make those inferences.

   - The *Making Inferences—Annotation Example* (page 58) can be used for your reference, to model annotating for students, or as an individual scaffold for students as necessary.

Close-Reading Skill—Making Inferences

Explain to students that to infer is to "read between the lines." Inferences can be made by asking questions while reading. Sometimes the answer is found directly in the text. When it is not, readers need to infer to determine the answer. Asking questions allows the reader to analyze and think critically about the text.

3. Assign the text-dependent questions on page 60. Students should accurately answer the questions, provide evidence (direct quotation or paraphrasing) from the reading passage to support their answers, include in-text citations with the (author and paragraph number), and write final thoughts to connect or further explain their answers.

Making Inferences—Annotation Example

①②③ = text evidence to be used in answers

Waiting and Watching
by Charles Victor

We have been waiting for many years. We wish to communicate <u>with these</u> <u>creatures of Earth,</u> whom we watch with fascination. Yet we must postpone our approach until they are ready.

This is vague- but "creatures" usually doesn't refer to humans

Over thousands of years, they have advanced. <u>First, they learned to farm.</u> Now, science is emerging. Finally, we are starting to see the first signs of the development we have been seeking.

Could this be a type of animal?

The Mayas are the first culture to give us real hope. Their math system is highly advanced, and they are the first Earthlings to discover the number zero. Their calculations become more complex each and every year that we observe them.

<u>Moreover, they understand the passing of time because they observe</u> the stars and planets. They, who recognize that <u>a year contains 365 days on Earth,</u> have developed a calendar to predict the seasons and time agriculture. ③

It seems the narrator is describing the timeline of humans

Their measurements are advanced, yet their interpretations are not. Despite all their years of observation, the Mayas still treat the stars and planets as if they are the same. They stay inside their homes when Venus rises in the morning, but they do not question why it acts differently than other "stars." They never ask how or why.

<u>They are a people to whom the stars are religion.</u> A priest charts the course and interprets the events. Rather than astronomy, the Mayas practice astrology. They do not seek to understand the heavens. They wish to know the ways the heavens will influence their lives.

How do we know if this is true or not?

Almost all the paragraphs have been about the solar system- is it someone from another planet?

Where we see the Milky Way, they see a road of souls who are traveling to the underworld from Earth. That underworld is a threat to the sun, which must pass through when it is out of sight at night. They feel they must satisfy evil gods, whose goal it is to stop the sun from rising again. To please these gods, the Mayas shed blood—their own and that of others. In their minds, these actions prevent the world from coming to an end.

The writer believes he is smarter than humans on Earth

<u>Although they still do not understand all they observe,</u> in Earth year AD 814, they are the most advanced of all the Earth's peoples. The civilizations that come after them will learn from their observations and continue to build their knowledge base. And ① many hundreds of years from now, the Earth may finally be populated with a <u>civilization we can approach.</u> Until then, we will <u>continue to watch and wait.</u>②

Making Inferences—"Waiting and Watching"

Directions: Read the text. Then, closely reread and annotate the text. In the margins, write any inferences you make and underline the text that helped you infer.

Close-Reading Tip

To infer is to "read between the lines." Good readers ask themselves questions about the text. Sometimes, these questions are answered as you read, and sometimes they are not. Asking questions allows you to analyze and critically think about the text as you read.

Waiting and Watching
by Charles Victor

We have been waiting for many years. We wish to communicate with these creatures of Earth, whom we watch with fascination. Yet we must postpone our approach until they are ready.

Over thousands of years, they have advanced. First, they learned to farm. Now, science is emerging. Finally, we are starting to see the first signs of the development we have been seeking.

The Mayas are the first culture to give us real hope. Their math system is highly advanced, and they are the first Earthlings to discover the number zero. Their calculations become more complex each and every year that we observe them.

Moreover, they understand the passing of time because they observe the stars and planets. They, who recognize that a year contains 365 days on Earth, have developed a calendar to predict the seasons and time agriculture.

Their measurements are advanced, yet their interpretations are not. Despite all their years of observation, the Mayas still treat the stars and planets as if they are the same. They stay inside their homes when Venus rises in the morning, but they do not question why it acts differently than other "stars." They never ask how or why.

They are a people to whom the stars are religion. A priest charts the course and interprets the events. Rather than astronomy, the Mayas practice astrology. They do not seek to understand the heavens. They wish to know the ways the heavens will influence their lives.

Where we see the Milky Way, they see a road of souls who are traveling to the underworld from Earth. That underworld is a threat to the sun, which must pass through when it is out of sight at night. They feel they must satisfy evil gods, whose goal it is to stop the sun from rising again. To please these gods, the Mayas shed blood—their own and that of others. In their minds, these actions prevent the world from coming to an end.

Although they still do not understand all they observe, in Earth year AD 814, they are the most advanced of all the Earth's peoples. The civilizations that come after them will learn from their observations and continue to build their knowledge base. And many hundreds of years from now, the Earth may finally be populated with a civilization we can approach. Until then, we will continue to watch and wait.

Name _____ Date _____

Making Inferences— "Waiting and Watching" *(cont.)*

Directions: Read "Waiting and Watching" on page 59, and respond to the questions.

Remember!

- Accurately answer the question by stating your claim.
- Provide evidence (direct quotation, block quotation, or paraphrasing) from the reading passage to support your answer.
- Include one in-text citation for each piece of evidence (author, paragraph number).
- Write a final thought to connect to or further elaborate on your answer.

1. What can you infer about who the narrator is? Use evidence to support your answer.

   _____

   _____

   _____

   _____

2. What does the narrator feel and/or think? What words from the text let you know this?

   _____

   _____

   _____

   _____

3. The narrator states, "The Mayas are the first culture to give us hope." Explain what this sentence means using textual evidence.

   _____

   _____

   _____

   _____

51701—Prove It! Using Textual Evidence   © *Shell Education*

Identifying Key Details

Materials

- *Identifying Key Details—Annotation Example* (page 62; page62.pdf) (optional)

- copies of *Identifying Key Details—Excerpt from "Sound Waves and Communication"* (pages 63–64; page63.pdf)

Procedure

1. Distribute *Identifying Key Details—Excerpt from "Sound Waves and Communication"* (pages 63–64). Have students read the passage independently.

2. Have students reread the passage, this time completing a close reading and annotation of the text. Students should focus on the close-reading skill of identifying key details.

   - The *Identifying Key Details—Annotation Example* (page 62) can be used for your reference, to model annotating for students, or as an individual scaffold for students as necessary.

Close-Reading Skill—Identifying Key Details

Have students underline key details. Students should determine which key details are essential to understanding the text. Tell students that if a detail can be left out of the passage without changing its meaning, it is not that important.

3. Assign the text-dependent questions on page 64. Students should accurately answer the question, provide evidence (direct quotation or paraphrasing) from the reading passage to support their answers, include in-text citations, and write final thoughts to connect or further explain their answers.

4. Remind students that a citation is needed directly following a quotation. In this case, the abbreviation *par.* is used to reference a specific paragraph.

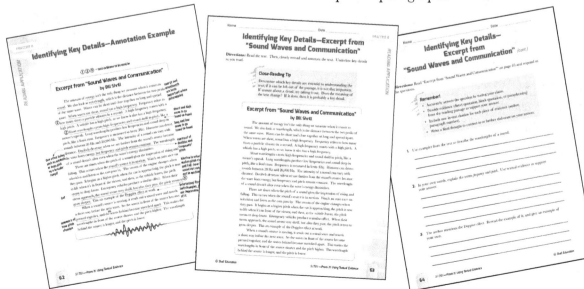

READING APPLICATION

Identifying Key Details—Annotation Example

①②③ = text evidence to be used in answers

Excerpt from "Sound Waves and Communication"
by Bill Shrill

The amount of energy isn't the only thing we measure when it comes to sound. We also look at wavelength, which is the distance between the two peaks of the same wave. Waves can be short and close together or long and spread apart. When waves are short, sound has a high frequency. Frequency refers to ② how many times a particle vibrates in a second. A high frequency comes with a high pitch. A whistle has a high pitch, so we know it also has a high frequency.

energy and wavelength are both important when determining how sound is measured

② Short wavelengths create high frequencies and sound shrill in pitch, like a mouse's squeak. Long wavelengths produce low frequencies and sound deep in pitch, like a lion's roar. Frequency is measured in hertz (Hz). Humans can detect sounds between 20 Hz and 20,000 Hz. The intensity of a sound can vary with distance. Decibels decrease when we are farther from the sound's source because the wave loses energy, but frequency and pitch remain constant. The wavelength of a sound doesn't alter even when the wave's energy diminishes.

short and high seem to go hand-in-hand

long and low seem to go hand-in-hand

Can other being such as animals or bugs pick up a broader range?

contrast of decibles and frequency/pitch

There are times when the pitch of a sound gives the impression of rising and falling. This occurs when the sound's source is in motion. Watch an auto race on television and listen as the cars pass by. The vroom of the engine changes when they pass. It begins at a higher pitch when the car is approaching, the pitch is true to life when it's in front of the viewer, and then, as the vehicle leaves, the pitch *but isn't?* seems to drop lower. Emergency vehicles produce a similar effect. When their sirens approach, the sound seems very shrill, but after they pass, the pitch seems to ③ grow deeper. This an example of the Doppler effect at work.

Motion is what makes pitch rise and fall- how is sound not ever not in motion?

Interesting! Pitch isn't changing, just our impression of it.

When a sound's source is moving, it sends out a sound wave and travels a short way before the next wave. So the waves in front of the source become *summary of how pitch changes* pressed together, and the waves behind become stretched apart. This makes the wavelengths in front of the source shorter and the pitch higher. The wavelength behind the source is longer, and the pitch is lower.

vs.

Identifying Key Details—Excerpt from "Sound Waves and Communication"

Directions: Read the text. Then, closely reread and annotate the text. Underline key details as you read.

Close-Reading Tip

Determine which key details are essential to understanding the text; if it can be left out of the passage, it is not that important. If unsure about a detail, try taking it out. Does the meaning of the text change? If it does, then it is probably a key detail.

Excerpt from "Sound Waves and Communication"
by Bill Shrill

The amount of energy isn't the only thing we measure when it comes to sound. We also look at wavelength, which is the distance between the two peaks of the same wave. Waves can be short and close together or long and spread apart. When waves are short, sound has a high frequency. Frequency refers to how many times a particle vibrates in a second. A high frequency comes with a high pitch. A whistle has a high pitch, so we know it also has a high frequency.

Short wavelengths create high frequencies and sound shrill in pitch, like a mouse's squeak. Long wavelengths produce low frequencies and sound deep in pitch, like a lion's roar. Frequency is measured in hertz (Hz). Humans can detect sounds between 20 Hz and 20,000 Hz. The intensity of a sound can vary with distance. Decibels decrease when we are farther from the sound's source because the wave loses energy, but frequency and pitch remain constant. The wavelength of a sound doesn't alter even when the wave's energy diminishes.

There are times when the pitch of a sound gives the impression of rising and falling. This occurs when the sound's source is in motion. Watch an auto race on television and listen as the cars pass by. The vroom of the engine changes when they pass. It begins at a higher pitch when the car is approaching, the pitch is true to life when it's in front of the viewer, and then, as the vehicle leaves, the pitch seems to drop lower. Emergency vehicles produce a similar effect. When their sirens approach, the sound seems very shrill, but after they pass, the pitch seems to grow deeper. This an example of the Doppler effect at work.

When a sound's source is moving, it sends out a sound wave and travels a short way before the next wave. So the waves in front of the source become pressed together, and the waves behind become stretched apart. This makes the wavelengths in front of the source shorter and the pitch higher. The wavelength behind the source is longer, and the pitch is lower.

READING APPLICATION

Identifying Key Details—
Excerpt from
"Sound Waves and Communication" *(cont.)*

Directions: Read "Excerpt from 'Sound Waves and Communication'" on page 63 and respond to the questions.

> ### Remember!
> - Accurately answer the question by stating your claim.
> - Provide evidence (direct quotation, block quotation, or paraphrasing) from the reading passage to support your answer.
> - Include one in-text citation for each piece of evidence (author, paragraph number).
> - Write a final thought to connect to or further elaborate on your answer.

1. Use examples from the text to describe the wavelengths of a sound.

   _____

   _____

   _____

2. In your own words, explain the terms *frequency* and *pitch*. Use textual evidence to support your answer.

   _____

   _____

   _____

3. The author mentions the Doppler effect. Reread the example of it, and give an example of your own.

   _____

   _____

   _____

Asking Questions

🖉 Materials

- *Asking Questions—Annotation Example* (page 66; page66.pdf) (optional)
- copies of *Asking Questions—"Tell Me Again, Dad"* (pages 67–68; page67.pdf)

Procedure

1. Distribute *Asking Questions—"Tell Me Again, Dad"* (pages 67–68). Have students read the passage independently.

2. Have students reread the passage, this time completing a close reading and annotation of the text. Students should focus specifically on the close-reading skill of asking questions.

   - The *Asking Questions—Annotation Example* (page 66) can be used for your reference, to model annotating for students, or as an individual scaffold for students as necessary.

Close-Reading Skill—Asking Questions

Have students read the questions prior to rereading the story. Have students annotate the text by writing questions they have as they read.

3. Assign the text-dependent questions on page 68. Explain to students that their responses should accurately answer the question, provide evidence (direct quotations, block quotations, or paraphrasing) from the reading passage to support the answers, include in-text citations, and conclude with final thoughts that connect or further explain the answers.

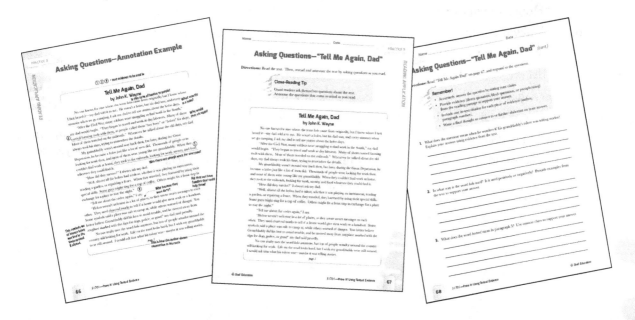

Asking Questions—Annotation Example

①②③ = text evidence to be used in answers

Tell Me Again, Dad
by John K. Wayne

Is this term offensive to people?

No one knows for sure where the term *hobo* came from originally, but I know where I first heard it—my dad told it to me. He wasn't a hobo, but his dad was, and every *What exactly is a hobo?* summer when we go camping, I ask my dad to tell me stories about the hobo days.

"After the Civil War, many soldiers were struggling to find work in the South," my dad would begin. "They began to travel and work as day laborers. Many of them *Why would they struggle?* ② carried farming tools with them, so people called them "hoe boys" or "hobos" for short. Most of them traveled on the railroads." Whenever he talked about the old days, my dad always took his time, trying to remember the details.

My granddaddy wasn't around way back then, but later, during the Great Depression, he became a hobo just like a lot of men did. Thousands of people were looking for work then, and most of them were young like my granddaddy. When they ① couldn't find work at home, they took to the railroads, looking for work, money, and food wherever they could find it.

Was there not enough work for everyone?

"How did they survive?" I always ask my dad.

"Well, almost all the hobos had a talent, whether it was playing an instrument, tending a garden, or repairing a fence. When they traveled, they bartered by using their special skills. Some guys might sing for a cup of coffee. Others might fix a front step in exchange for a place to stay the night." ③

Did they not have families that could help them?

"Tell me about the codes again," I say.

Why because they were dirty?

"Hobos weren't welcome in a lot of places, so they wrote secret messages to each other. They used charcoal marks to tell if a home would give men work or a handout. Some symbols said a place was safe to camp at, while others warned of danger. You *This reminds me of houses being marked in the Underground Railroad.* better believe Granddaddy did his best to avoid trouble, and he steered away from anyplace marked with the sign for dogs, police, or guns!" my dad said proudly.

This is how the author shows connection to his roots

No one really uses the word *hobo* anymore, but lots of people wander around the country still looking for work. Life on the road looks hard, but I wish my granddaddy were still around. I would ask him what his talent was—maybe it was telling stories.

page 1

Asking Questions—"Tell Me Again, Dad"

Directions: Read the text. Then, reread and annotate the text by asking questions as you read.

Close-Reading Tip

Good readers ask themselves questions about the text. Annotate the questions that come to mind as you read.

Tell Me Again, Dad
by John K. Wayne

No one knows for sure where the term *hobo* came from originally, but I know where I first heard it—my dad told it to me. He wasn't a hobo, but his dad was, and every summer when we go camping, I ask my dad to tell me stories about the hobo days.

"After the Civil War, many soldiers were struggling to find work in the South," my dad would begin. "They began to travel and work as day laborers. Many of them carried farming tools with them. Most of them traveled on the railroads." Whenever he talked about the old days, my dad always took his time, trying to remember the details.

My granddaddy wasn't around way back then, but later, during the Great Depression, he became a hobo just like a lot of men did. Thousands of people were looking for work then, and most of them were young like my granddaddy. When they couldn't find work at home, they took to the railroads, looking for work, money, and food wherever they could find it.

"How did they survive?" I always ask my dad.

"Well, almost all the hobos had a talent, whether it was playing an instrument, tending a garden, or repairing a fence. When they traveled, they bartered by using their special skills. Some guys might sing for a cup of coffee. Others might fix a front step in exchange for a place to stay the night."

"Tell me about the codes again," I say.

"Hobos weren't welcome in a lot of places, so they wrote secret messages to each other. They used charcoal marks to tell if a home would give men work or a handout. Some symbols said a place was safe to camp at, while others warned of danger. You better believe Granddaddy did his best to avoid trouble, and he steered away from anyplace marked with the sign for dogs, police, or guns!" my dad said proudly.

No one really uses the word *hobo* anymore, but lots of people wander around the country still looking for work. Life on the road looks hard, but I wish my granddaddy were still around. I would ask him what his talent was—maybe it was telling stories.

page 1

Asking Questions—"Tell Me Again, Dad" *(cont.)*

Directions: Read "Tell Me Again Dad" on page 67, and respond to the questions.

Remember!

- Accurately answer the question by stating your claim.
- Provide evidence (direct quotation, block quotation, or paraphrasing) from the reading passage to support your answer.
- Include one in-text citation for each piece of evidence (author, paragraph number).
- Write a final thought to connect to or further elaborate on your answer.

1. What does the narrator mean when he wonders if his granddaddy's talent was telling stories? Explain your answer using evidence from the text.

   _____

   _____

   _____

   _____

2. In what way is the word *hobo* used? Is it used positively or negatively? Provide examples from the text to support your answer.

   _____

   _____

   _____

   _____

3. What does the word *bartered* mean in paragraph 5? Use context clues to support your answer.

   _____

   _____

   _____

   _____

Compare and Contrast

✏ Materials

- *Compare and Contrast—Annotation Example* (page 70; page70.pdf) (optional)
- copies of *Compare and Contrast—"The Nutrient Cycle"* (pages 71–72; page71.pdf)
- colored pencils or pens

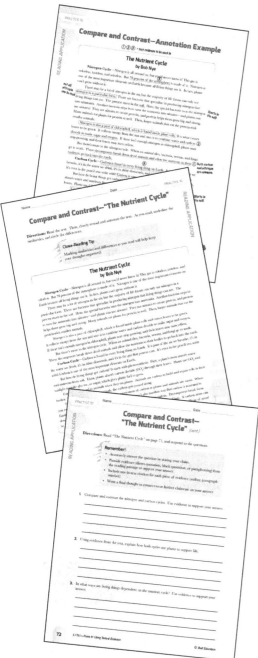

Procedure

1. Distribute *Compare and Contrast—"The Nutrient Cycle"* (pages 71–72). Explain to students that as they read, they will be identifying similarities and differences.

2. Have students closely read the passage, underlining similarities and circling differences as they read.

   - The *Compare and Contrast—Annotation Example* (page 70) can be used for your reference, to model annotating for students, or as an individual scaffold for students as necessary.

3. Have students create two-column charts labeled "Compare" and "Contrast." Students should write the information they underlined or circled under the appropriate heading. This will make it easier to identify information to use in answers.

Close-Reading Skill—Compare and Contrast

Explain to students that comparing and contrasting is finding the similarities and differences between two or more texts. Using different colored pens or pencils will help keep their thoughts organized.

4. Assign the text-dependent questions on page 72. Explain to students that their responses should accurately answer the question, provide evidence (direct quotations, block quotations, or paraphrasing) from the reading passage to support the answers, include in-text citations, and conclude with final thoughts that connect or further explain the answers.

5. Remind students that a citation is needed directly following a quotation. In this case, the abbreviation *par.* is used to reference a specific paragraph.

READING APPLICATION

Compare and Contrast—Annotation Example

①②③ = text evidence to be used in answers

The Nutrient Cycle
by Bob Nye

Nitrogen Cycle—Nitrogen is all around us, but you'd never know it! This gas is colorless, tasteless, and odorless. But 78 percent of the atmosphere is made of it. Nitrogen is one of the most important elements on Earth because all living things use it. In fact, plants can't grow without it.
③

There may be a lot of nitrogen in the air, but the majority of life forms can only use nitrogen in a particular form. There are bacteria that specialize in producing nitrogen that living things can use. The process starts in the soil. Here, the special bacteria turn the nitrogen into ammonia. Another bacteria steps in to turn the ammonia into nitrates—and plants can use nitrates! They use nitrates to create protein, and protein helps them grow big and strong. Many animals eat plants for protein as well. Then, larger animals that eat the protein-rich smaller animals.

not all nitrogen can be used

Starts in the soil!

Different- found inside plant cells

Nitrogen is also a part of chlorophyll, which is found inside plant cells. It is what causes leaves to be green. It collects energy from the sun and uses it to combine water and carbon ② dioxide to make sugar and oxygen. If there isn't enough nitrogen in chlorophyll, plants may stop growing, and their leaves may turn yellow.

But there's more to the nitrogen cycle. When an animal dies, bacteria, worms, and fungi go to work. These decomposers break down dead animals and allow the nutrients in their ① bodies to go back into the earth. ③

Both carbon and nitrogen are common

Carbon Cycle—Carbon is found in every living thing on Earth. It is part of the air we breathe, it's in the water we drink, it's in shiny diamonds, and it's in the gas that powers cars. It's even in the pencil you write with! Carbon is one of the most important elements on Earth.

But how do living things get carbon? It starts with photosynthesis. First, a plant's roots absorb water and nutrients from soil. Then, plants absorb carbon dioxide (CO_2) through their leaves. Plants use CO_2 and sunlight to make glucose, or sugar, which gives plants fuel to grow.

carbon and nitrogen both claim to be important elements

Starts in the soil!

Carbon gets passed to animals when they eat plants. Animals use carbon to build and ② repair cells in their bodies. When animals eat other animals, the carbon gets passed along.

The carbon cycle doesn't just involve the movement of carbon as plants and animals are eaten. When you exhale, you return carbon dioxide into the air. But there's also another way that carbon is returned to Earth. When plants and the animals that eat them die, they also release carbon. Decomposers break them down and return carbon to the soil. Then, the carbon can be used by more living things. A carbon atom can be used again and again. It recycles itself and can be part of many different organisms over millions of years!

We release carbon dioxide out of or bodies

Both are returned to the Earth in the soil by decomposition

Compare and Contrast—"The Nutrient Cycle"

Directions: Read the text. Then, closely reread and annotate the text. As you read, underline the similarities, and circle the differences.

Close-Reading Tip

Marking similarities and differences as you read will help keep your thoughts organized.

The Nutrient Cycle
by Bob Nye

Nitrogen Cycle—Nitrogen is all around us, but you'd never know it! This gas is colorless, tasteless, and odorless. But 78 percent of the atmosphere is made of it. Nitrogen is one of the most important elements on Earth because all living things use it. In fact, plants can't grow without it.

There may be a lot of nitrogen in the air, but the majority of life forms can only use nitrogen in a particular form. There are bacteria that specialize in producing nitrogen that living things can use. The process starts in the soil. Here, the special bacteria turn the nitrogen into ammonia. Another bacteria steps in to turn the ammonia into nitrates—and plants can use nitrates! They use nitrates to create protein, and protein helps them grow big and strong. Many animals eat plants for protein as well. Then, larger animals that eat the protein-rich smaller animals.

Nitrogen is also a part of chlorophyll, which is found inside plant cells and causes leaves to be green. It collects energy from the sun and uses it to combine water and carbon dioxide to make sugar and oxygen. If there isn't enough nitrogen in chlorophyll, plants may stop growing, and their leaves may turn yellow.

But there's more to the nitrogen cycle. When an animal dies, bacteria, worms, and fungi go to work. These decomposers break down dead animals and allow the nutrients in their bodies to go back into the earth.

Carbon Cycle—Carbon is found in every living thing on Earth. It is part of the air we breathe, it's in the water we drink, it's in shiny diamonds, and it's in the gas that powers cars. It's even in the pencil you write with! Carbon is one of the most important elements on Earth.

But how do living things get carbon? It starts with photosynthesis. First, a plant's roots absorb water and nutrients from soil. Then, plants absorb carbon dioxide (CO_2) through their leaves. Plants use CO_2 and sunlight to make glucose, or sugar, which gives plants fuel to grow.

Carbon gets passed to animals when they eat plants. Animals use carbon to build and repair cells in their bodies. When animals eat other animals, the carbon gets passed along.

The carbon cycle doesn't just involve the movement of carbon as plants and animals are eaten. When you exhale, you return carbon dioxide into the air. But there's also another way that carbon is returned to Earth. When plants and the animals that eat them die, they also release carbon. Decomposers break them down and return carbon to the soil. Then, the carbon can be used by more living things. A carbon atom can be used again and again. It recycles itself and can be part of many different organisms over millions of years!

Name _____ Date _____

Compare and Contrast— "The Nutrient Cycle" (cont.)

Directions: Read "The Nutrient Cycle" on page 71, and respond to the questions.

Remember!
- Accurately answer the question by stating your claim.
- Provide evidence (direct quotation, block quotation, or paraphrasing) from the reading passage to support your answer.
- Include one in-text citation for each piece of evidence (author, paragraph number).
- Write a final thought to connect to or further elaborate on your answer.

1. Compare and contrast the nitrogen and carbon cycles. Use evidence to support your answer.

   _____

   _____

   _____

   _____

2. Using evidence from the text, explain how both cycles use plants to support life.

   _____

   _____

   _____

   _____

3. In what ways are living things dependent on the nutrient cycle? Use evidence to support your answer.

   _____

   _____

   _____

   _____

Writing Lessons and Application

Textual Evidence in Writing

Writing Application Prompts

Using Credible and Reliable Sources

🔍 Objective

Students will search for and gather credible and reliable sources for research.

✏️ Materials

- copies of *Using Credible and Reliable Sources Practice 1* (page 76; page76.pdf)
- copies of *Using Credible and Reliable Sources Practice 2* (page 77; page77.pdf)

💡 Essential Question

How do I gather credible and reliable sources for research?

Additional Support

Allow extra time for students to practice visiting reliable and unreliable websites to compare and contrast the differences.

Guided Practice

1. Distribute copies of *Using Credible and Reliable Sources Practice 1* (page 76). Begin by defining what a source is (a text that you can use to read about a topic) and explaining the differences between print and digital sources. Have students write these definitions on their activity sheets.

2. Students should understand that they can look for sources on the Internet about a topic, but they should be careful. Some things will not be what they are looking for, and some will not be reliable (able to be trusted; typically supported by experts) or credible (true; able to be believed). Students should write these definitions on their activity sheets.

3. Explain that finding credible and reliable sources is key when using text evidence. Tell students that one way to prove if a source is reliable and credible is to check the information using more than one source.

4. Tell students that when they need to do research, they should type in key words to find what they need. They should only type in the main key words about their topics. Help students complete numbers 5–7 on page 76.

5. Remind students that when searching the Internet, they should look for reliable and credible sources. Websites such as blogs, Wikipedia, or social media would not be good sources. Websites such as encyclopedias or other expert websites would be good sources.

6. Have students look at the list of options that could come up when searching for "getting a passport." Go through each option with students, and discuss which websites would be reliable and credible and which would not by writing "Yes" or "No" next to each number.

7. Explain to students that they should never click on websites that require them to be a certain age, that have inappropriate material, or that ask them to give personal information.

Independent Practice

- Have students complete the *Using Credible and Reliable Sources Practice 2* (page 77) in class, as homework, or as an assessment to ensure they can complete the skill independently.

Name _____   Date _____

Using Credible and Reliable Sources Practice 1

Directions: Define the vocabulary words related to the word *sources*.

1. print source: _____

2. digital source: _____

3. reliable source: _____

4. credible source: _____

Directions: Which keywords would you use to search for the topic described?

5. You want to find out about what you need to know to adopt a llama.

   _____

6. You want to find out how to make homemade slime.

   _____

7. You want to know how to get a passport to travel the world.

   _____

Directions: State which sources appear to be both reliable and credible by writing "Yes" or "No" next to each example.

_____ 8. **www.passports.org**
                    Find out what your country requires to get any type of passport. Provided here are the applications and…

_____ 9. **www.bloggingaroundtheworld.com**
                    I used my passport to go to BRAZIL! The best trip EVER! We ate and ate and ate until we were stuffed…

_____ 10. **www.howtotravel.net/getapassport**
                    To get a passport, you first need to go to a government website and see what the general requirements are…

_____ 11. **www.quickpassports.com**
                    Send us your social security number and we will guarantee your passport in less than 48 hours. Australia, here you come!

_____ 12. **www.unitedstatesgovernment.gov/passports**
                    Applications / Fees / Types / Documents Needed: Click here to Apply for or Renew your passport in person or by mail…

Using Credible and Reliable Sources Practice 2

Directions: Write in the keywords you would use to search for the topic described.

1. You want to research what countries were involved in World War I:

   _____

2. You want to find out what you need to make a homemade facial mask:

   _____

3. You want to find out about the strangest mammals in the United States:

   _____

4. You want to find the best new apps for filtering photos:

   _____

5. You want to find out the largest mountains in the world:

   _____

Directions: State which sources appear to be both reliable and credible about the largest mountains in the world by writing "Yes" or "No" next to each example.

_____ 6. **www.climbmounteverest.org**
Learn everything you need to know to prepare to climb one of the most dangerous mountains in the world!

_____ 7. **www.todaysnews.com**
Steve Jacks reports on the largest mountains as of today, and which are safe to climb for those of you who are adventurous…

_____ 8. **www.mountainsrus.com**
See the most beautiful mountains in the world as we explore the ins and outs of what makes a mountain incredible.

Tip: Be sure your sources are reliable and credible. If you are unsure, check at least two additional sources to see if the information matches. If it doesn't, that source is probably not reliable and/or credible.

Supporting a Claim

🔍 Objective

Students will understand how to support a claim by drawing relevant evidence and using logical reasoning.

✏️ Materials

- copies of *Supporting a Claim Practice 1* (page 79; page79.pdf)
- copies of *Supporting a Claim Practice 2* (page 80; page80.pdf)

💡 Essential Question

How do I support a claim using logical reasoning and relevant evidence?

Guided Practice

1. Begin by explaining that when you make a claim about a topic, you should have arguments that what you are saying holds value. You do this by supporting your claim with logical reasoning and relevant evidence.
   - Logical reasoning is statement that makes a claim make sense.
   - Relevant evidence is facts that come from sources.
2. Have students imagine they are going to write about whether video games should be considered a sport.
3. Distribute *Supporting a Claim Practice 1* (page 79). Have students read each example and follow the directions. As a class, talk through each example and guide students to better understand how to support a claim.
4. Explain to students that although a sentence sometimes does not have logical reasoning or relevant evidence, it is still useful to include, such as a topic statement.
5. Explain to students that they should not rely only on logical reasoning or relevant evidence, but should also use their own background knowledge on the subject to support their claims.

Independent Practice

- Have students complete *Supporting a Claim Practice 2* (page 80) in class, as homework, or as an assessment to ensure they can complete the skill independently.

Additional Support

Give students a list of reliable online sources to use or encourage them to go to local libraries and find reliable printed sources.

Supporting a Claim Practice 1

Directions: Read the text. Then, for each statement, fill in the line using the correct letters:

LR—Logical Reasoning   **RE—Relevant Evidence**   **N—Neither**

Should Bottle Flipping Be Considered a Sport?

Bottle flipping may be a new "sport." Taking a partially filled water bottle and flipping it in the air to land upright is the goal of the game. This takes a good balance of both skill and practice as well as just the right amount of water. What started as a simple talent show act in 2016 has ripened into a common practice in cafeterias as well as a viral Internet obsession. Bottle flipping competitions are held informally every day among school-age children. Formal competitions have also been held across the country, and there is even a petition to add it as an Olympic sport! Perhaps with all this publicity, it will be the new sport of the decade!

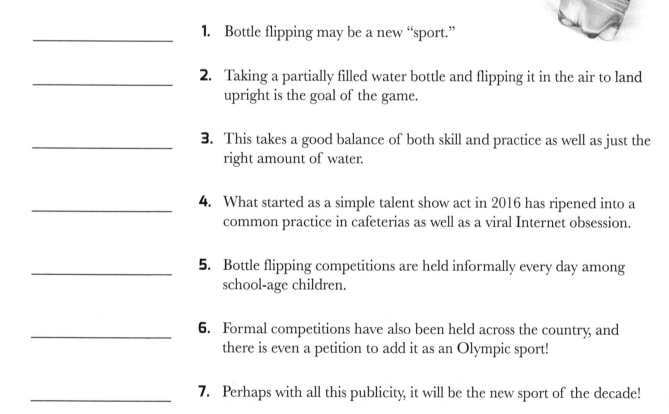

_____ **1.** Bottle flipping may be a new "sport."

_____ **2.** Taking a partially filled water bottle and flipping it in the air to land upright is the goal of the game.

_____ **3.** This takes a good balance of both skill and practice as well as just the right amount of water.

_____ **4.** What started as a simple talent show act in 2016 has ripened into a common practice in cafeterias as well as a viral Internet obsession.

_____ **5.** Bottle flipping competitions are held informally every day among school-age children.

_____ **6.** Formal competitions have also been held across the country, and there is even a petition to add it as an Olympic sport!

_____ **7.** Perhaps with all this publicity, it will be the new sport of the decade!

Supporting a Claim Practice 2

Directions: Read the text. Then, for each statement, fill in the line using the correct letters:

LR—Logical Reasoning   **RE—Relevant Evidence**   **N—Neither**

Should Graffiti be Considered Art?

Art is considered an expression of imagination. If this is true, then graffiti should be considered an art. Graffiti is problematic for workers to clean up. Workers don't get compensated very well to clean it off cement walls. For a long time, graffiti was considered threatening and unattractive, but looks are opinion based! Graffiti involves more than just words, and it dates back to the prehistoric times of cavemen. Graffiti can be a symbol of the people on the streets, and sometimes can send positive messages of love and community. Many people are trained in certain types of graffiti, and classes can be found at local community colleges about graffiti.

_____ **1.** Art is considered an expression of imagination.

_____ **2.** If this is true, then graffiti should be considered an art.

_____ **3.** Graffiti is problematic for workers to clean up.

_____ **4.** Workers don't get compensated very well to clean it off cement walls.

_____ **5.** For a long time, graffiti was considered threatening and unattractive, but looks are opinion based!

_____ **6.** Graffiti involves more than just words, and it dates back to the prehistoric times of cavemen.

_____ **7.** Graffiti can be a symbol of the people on the streets, and sometimes can send positive messages of love and community.

_____ **8.** Many people are trained in certain types of graffiti, and classes can be found at local community colleges about graffiti.

Tip: Remember that logical reasoning is a statement makes a claim make sense. Relevant evidence is a fact that supports a claim from an outside source.

Organizing Evidence

🔍 Objective

Students will organize evidence into categories before beginning writing.

✏️ Materials

- copies of *Organizing Evidence Practice 1* (page 82; page82.pdf)
- copies of *Organizing Evidence Practice 2* (page 83; page83.pdf)

💡 Essential Question

How do I organize my research into categories for prewriting?

Guided Practice

1. Explain to students that when you are writing about a topic and have claims to support that topic, you should organize the facts and opinions into categories so your writing is organized.

2. Tell students they will read a list of statements on stopping the elimination of art classes from school curriculum. Each of the statements will be either logical reasoning or relevant evidence. Have students categorize these topics into three main categories about the topic, "Arts Classes in Schools Should Stay!"

3. Distribute copies of *Organizing Evidence Practice 1* (page 82). Have students read through the statements and come up with logical categories.

4. Explain to students that they should not simply list facts as support in the order that they think of them or find them but that claims should always be organized into bigger categories that have evidence to back them up.

Independent Practice

- Have students complete *Organizing Evidence Practice 2* (page 83) in class, as homework, or as an assessment to ensure they can complete the skill independently.

Additional Support

Have students highlight information and write a letter or number next to the text to represent each category.

Name _____ Date _____

Organizing Evidence Practice 1

Directions: Read each note about keeping art classes in schools. Then, come up with ways the statements could be categorized into three main topics. Rewrite each note in the correct column of the chart.

Art Classes Should Stay!

- *Unlike any other subject, art allows expression of your emotions.*
- *Students learn the basics of art history.*
- *Specific skills are learned in relation to perspective, shading, and color.*
- *Art teaches about the background of other cultures.*
- *Art can be therapeutic for students and help them de-stress.*
- *Art is part of development of fine motor skills.*
- *Students can learn about famous artists.*
- *Art is in many jobs of the future and helps creativity flow.*
- *Art is one of the few subjects that comes without parameters.*

Topic A: _____	Topic B: _____	Topic C: _____

Organizing Evidence Practice 2

Directions: Read each statement about Bob Marley. Then, come up with ways they could be categorized into three main topics, and list the topics in the boxes. Rewrite each note in the correct column of the chart.

The Life of Bob Marley

- Marley made several trips to Africa to help oppressed people.
- Marley was born February 6, 1945.
- Marley helped his own country of Jamaica and received the Order of Merit.
- Marley worked a lot with Johnny Nash.
- Marley was born and raised in Jamaica.
- Marley was awarded the Medal of Peace from the United Nations for his work.
- Marley played a type of music called reggae.
- Marley died May 11, 1981.
- Marley played with a band named Bob Marley and the Wailers.

Topic A: _____	Topic B: _____	Topic C: _____

Tip: Remember that the facts should be organized into similar topics before writing begins so that the writing will make sense to the reader.

Writing an Analysis

🔍 Objective

Students will write organized and supported analyses using textual evidence from a text.

✏️ Materials

- copies of *Writing an Analysis Practice 1* (page 85; page85.pdf)
- copies of *Writing an Analysis Practice 2* (page 86; page86.pdf)

💡 Essential Question

How do I put together an organized and supported analysis of a topic?

Guided Practice

1. Explain to students that they will be researching the question, "What is courage?" Students will use digital sources to choose attributes that define courage.

2. To organize their essays, students should have five paragraphs. The first should be two to three sentences stating the topic. The next three paragraphs should discuss the attributes of courage and should include explanations, examples, and details. Then, the final paragraph should conclude with a summary of the topic in two to three sentences. (It would be a good idea to draw this organization on the board, so students can see how to organize their essays throughout the practice time.)

3. Distribute *Writing an Analysis Practice 1* (page 85). Students will use the graphic organizer to take notes from their research (to later be used with a text citation) as well as their own logical reasoning. Students will use these notes to organize their writing before they write their essay on *Writing an Analysis Practice 2* (page 86).

4. Provide students time to research and organize their findings into three main topics or attributes.

5. Explain to students that they should not include everything from their research. Instead, they should use evidence that will most clearly explain their three main attributes for what courage is. Remind students they should use exact words and phrases from the text as part of their evidence. They should have a minimum of one in-text citation from a reliable source in each of the three main paragraphs of the body.

Independent Practice

- Have students complete *Writing and Analysis Practice 2* (page 86) in class, as homework, or as an assessment.

Additional Support

Assist students in coming up with category ideas *(feeling scared but doing it anyway, standing up for what you think is right, facing bravery in difficult circumstances)*.

Name _____ Date _____

Writing an Analysis Practice 1

Directions: Use the Internet to research the question, *What is courage?* Use the graphic organizer to take notes and organize your findings. Be sure each main topic includes logical reasoning and relevant evidence.

What Is Courage?

Topic Summary		
1st Main Topic (one attribute of courage)	**2nd Main Topic** (one attribute of courage)	**3rd Main Topic** (one attribute of courage)
Details	**Details**	**Details**

Summative Conclusion

INDEPENDENT PRACTICE

Writing an Analysis Practice 2

Directions: Use the graphic organizer from page 85 to write a five-paragraph essay answering the question, *What is courage?*

_____

_____

_____

_____

_____

_____

_____

_____

_____

_____

_____

_____

_____

_____

_____

_____

Tip: Remember that your three body paragraphs should stay on topic with the three main attributes that define courage. Use at least one quotation with in-text citations for each of the main topics.

Creating a Bibliography

Objective

Students will list sources from the in-text citations in their writing as a bibliography (also called works cited or references). **Note:** *Talk to your local curriculum director to find which preferred style would be most applicable for your students.*

Materials

- copies of *Creating a Bibliography Practice 1* (page 88; page88.pdf)
- copies of *Creating a Bibliography Practice 2* (page 89; page89.pdf)

Essential Question

How do I create a bibliography at the end of my writing?

Guided Practice

1. Explain to students that when they write essays, they must each create a list of sources they used to help write their papers. In MLA format, the list should be titled Bibliography and should include the sources in alphabetical order by the authors' last names. While listing sources in MLA style is more thorough, the list can be simplified as needed.

Bibliography

Book	Author Last Name, First Name. *Title.* Publisher.
Encyclopedia or other article	Author Last Name, First Name. "Title." *Name of Magazine* or Publisher.
Online source	Author or website creator (if found). "Title of Article." *Main Website Name.* URL.

2. Distribute *Creating a Bibliography Practice 1* (page 88). Have students practice creating bibliographies by using the sources shown in the graphics. Assist students in completing the sources list as needed.

Independent Practice

- Have students complete *Creating a Bibliography Practice 2* (page 89) in class, as homework, or as an assessment to ensure they can complete the skill independently.

Additional Support

Students who need additional support may need to name out loud each component of the entry (i.e., author last name, author first name).

Creating a Bibliography Practice 1

Directions: Pretend you wrote an essay about interesting hobbies. Create bibliography listings using the sources provided.

The Best Hobbies of the 21st Century
By Steve Player
Crater Publishing

_____

_____

_____

Hobbies You Can Do
By Julie Flyer
Outdoor Adventure Magazine

_____

_____

_____

www.hobbies.com
Exploring the World Through Hobbies
By Barb Hiker

_____

_____

_____

Creating a Bibliography Practice 2

Directions: Pretend you wrote an essay about how different parts of the world make pizza, and used the sources below. Write out the listing for each source. Then, on a separate sheet of paper, rewrite them in alphabetical order.

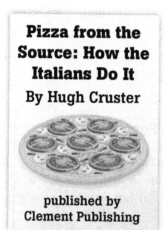

Pizza from the Source: How the Italians Do It
By Hugh Cruster

published by Clement Publishing

_____

_____

_____

Best Pizza Recipes in Mexico
By Jose Clinger

Chef At Home Magazine

_____

_____

_____

www.recipesfromearth.com

Pizza Around the Globe
By Vivian Trail

_____

_____

_____

Tip: Remember that a bibliography should go in alphabetical order by the authors' last names.

Description Text Structure

✏️ Materials

- copies of *"A Fork in Time"* (pages 91–92; page91.pdf)

Procedure

1. Distribute *"A Fork in Time"* (pages 91–92). Have students read the prompt related to the article. The prompt is: *Using textual evidence, examine how and why Americans began changing the way the fork was used.*

2. Have students read the text independently and think about how they will respond to the prompt.

Student Annotation Focus

While students read, have them annotate by underlining the important information about the use of forks throughout history and writing notes and questions in the margins.

3. Have students read the text and annotate as directed.

4. Tell students to use the information from the text to respond to the prompt. You may choose to allow each student to use an additional credible source.

5. Remind students to use quotations, paraphrasing, and textual evidence and citations. Remind students that a citation is needed directly following a quotation. In this case, the abbreviation *par.* is used to reference a specific paragraph.

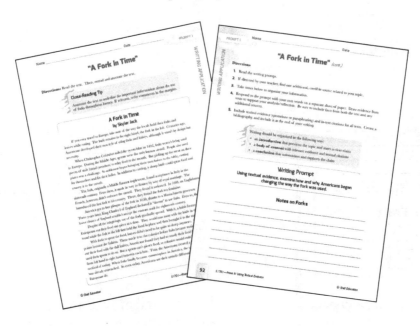

Name _____   Date _____

"A Fork In Time"

Directions: Read the text. Then, reread and annotate the text.

Close-Reading Tip

Annotate the text to underline the important information about the use of forks throughout history. If relevant, write comments in the margins.

A Fork in Time
by Skyler Jack

If you ever travel to Europe, take note of the way the locals hold their forks and knives while eating. The knife remains in the right hand, the fork in the left. Centuries ago, Americans developed their own style of using forks and knives, although it wasn't by design but necessity.

When Christopher Columbus sailed the ocean blue in 1492, forks weren't being used in Europe. During the Middle Ages, spoons were the only known utensil. People also used pieces of stale bread (trenchers) to relay food to the mouth. But picking up the meat on their plates was a challenge. So noblemen began bringing their own knives to the table, cutting for themselves and for their ladies. In addition to cutting, a sharp knife could spear food and convey it to the mouth.

The fork, originally a Middle Eastern implement, found acceptance in Italy in the sixteenth century. From there, it made its way to France by way of royal marriage. The French, however, didn't embrace the utensil. They found it awkward. In 1608, an Englishman introduced the first fork to his country. There, they found the fork too feminine.

America got its first glimpse of the fork in 1630, thanks to a Massachusetts governor. Three years later, King Charles I of England declared it "decent" to use forks. Even so, the lower classes of England wouldn't accept the custom until the eighteenth century.

Despite all the misgivings, use of the fork gradually spread. With it, a habit formed: Europeans cut their food one piece at a time. They would saw away with the knife in the right hand while the fork in the left first held the food in place and then brought it to the mouth.

With forks to spear the food, knives didn't need to be quite so sharp anymore. Duller points became the fashion. These made it to the colonies before forks became mainstream. To cut their food with the dull knives, Americans found they had to steady their food first. They used their spoon to do so. But a spoon can't pierce food, so colonists would switch the spoon from left hand to right hand between each bite. Thus, the Americans created a "zigzag" method of eating. When forks finally became commonplace in America, the zigzag habit was already entrenched. So even today, Americans use their utensils differently from the way Europeans do.

Name _____ Date _____

"A Fork in Time" *(cont.)*

Directions

1. Read the writing prompt.

2. If directed by your teacher, find one additional, credible source related to your topic.

3. Take notes below to organize your information.

4. Respond to the prompt with your own words on a separate sheet of paper. Draw evidence from texts to support your analysis/reflection. Be sure to include facts from both the text and any additional sources.

5. Include textual evidence (quotations or paraphrasing) and in-text citations for all texts. Create a bibliography, and include it at the end of your writing.

Writing should be organized in the following way:

- an **introduction** that previews the topic and states a clear claim
- a **body of content** with relevant evidence and textual citations
- a **conclusion** that summarizes and supports the claim

Writing Prompt

Using textual evidence, examine how and why Americans began changing the way the fork was used.

Notes on Forks

_____

_____

_____

_____

_____

_____

Compare and Contrast Text Structure

Materials

- copies of *"The Writing on the Wall"* (pages 94–95; page94.pdf)

Procedure

1. Distribute *"The Writing on the Wall"* (pages 94–95). Have students read the prompt related to the passage. The prompt is: *Are you for or against street art? Explain your reasoning using textual evidence.*

2. Have students read the text independently and think about how they will answer the prompt.

Student Annotation Focus

While students read, have them underline the reasons street art may be construed as good, circle negative effects of the art, and annotate by writing notes and questions in the margins.

3. Have students read the text and annotate as directed.

4. Tell students to use the information from the text to respond to the prompt. You may choose to allow each student to use an additional credible source.

5. Remind students to follow the directions and to use textual evidence and citations.

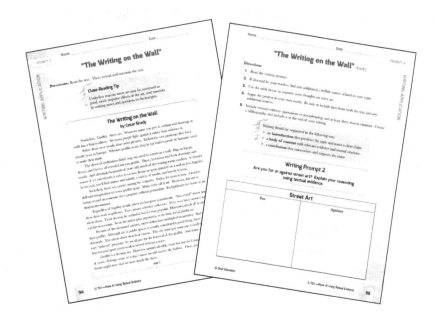

"The Writing on the Wall"

Directions: Read the text. Then, reread and annotate the text.

Close-Reading Tip

Underline reasons street art may be construed as good, circle negative effects of the art, and annotate by writing notes and questions in the margins.

The Writing on the Wall
by Cesar Brady

Vandalism. Graffiti. Street art. Whatever name you give it, writing and drawing on walls has a long tradition. Yet many people fight against it rather than embrace it.

Before there were words, there were pictures. Prehistoric cave paintings date back 40,000 years in Europe. Whether graffiti or art, they're our earliest proof of humans' need to make their mark.

The dawn of civilization didn't stop our need to scrawl on a wall. Digs in Egypt, Rome, and Greece all revealed ancient graffiti. There, historians find both drawings and words. And although thousands of years old, much of the writing seems modern. It doesn't matter if it's carved with a stylus in ancient Rome or spray-painted on a wall in Los Angeles. In the mix, you'll find names and initials, a variety of insults, and bawdy humor.

Back then, there was poetry among the vulgarity. Today, the same is true. Creative skill and imagination set some graffiti apart. Many even call it art. However, this art is being created on someone else's property without permission. It's legitimate art made in an illegitimate manner.

Regardless of legality or risk, street art has gone mainstream. "Successful" street artists show their work in galleries. They attract celebrity collectors. They even have movies made about them. Their art may be unlawful, but it's very popular. Moreover, much of it carries a political message. So as the artists gain popularity, so do their social platforms.

Because of the increased interest, street artists have multiplied in number. And so has their graffiti. Although art in public spaces is usually considered a good thing, there's also a downside. The artists don't own their canvas. The city must pay someone to buff or paint over "defaced" property. So we all pay for the removal of the graffiti. And some artists and fans become upset when work is erased without a trace.

Graffiti is a fleeting art. However, against all odds, some has survived many thousands of years. Perhaps some of today's street art will survive the buffers. Then, people of the future might note that we were much like them.

page 1

51701—Prove It! Using Textual Evidence

"The Writing on the Wall" *(cont.)*

Directions

1. Read the writing prompt.

2. If directed by your teacher, find one additional, credible source related to your topic.

3. Use the table below to organize your thoughts on street art.

4. Argue the prompt in your own words. Be sure to include facts from both the text and any additional sources.

5. Include textual evidence (quotations or paraphrasing) and at least three in-text citations. Create a bibliography, and include it at the end of your writing.

Writing should be organized in the following way:

- an **introduction** that previews the topic and states a clear claim
- a **body of content** with relevant evidence and textual citations
- a **conclusion** that summarizes and supports the claim

Writing Prompt 2

Are you for or against street art? Explain your reasoning using textual evidence.

Street Art	
For	**Against**

WRITING APPLICATION

Cause-and-Effect Text Structure

✏️ Materials

- copies of *"A Smart Move"* (pages 97–98; page97.pdf)

Procedure

1. Distribute *"A Smart Move"* (pages 97–98). Have students read the prompt related to the passage. The prompt is: *Use details from the text to explain two ways exercise can help students academically.*

2. Have students read the text independently and think about how they will respond to the prompt.

Student Annotation Focus

While students read, have them underline facts about exercise. Encourage students to write comments in the margins about exercise increasing student attention and focus.

3. Have students reread the text and annotate as directed.

4. Have students use the information from the text to respond to the prompt. You may choose to allow each student to use one additional credible source.

5. Remind students to follow the directions and to use textual evidence and citations.

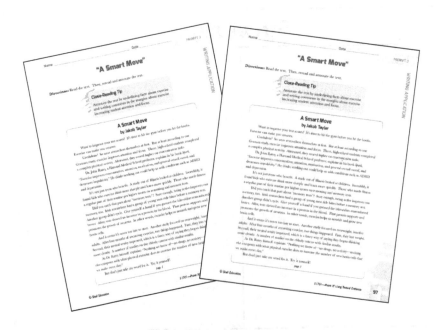

"A Smart Move"

Directions: Read the text. Then, reread and annotate the text.

Close-Reading Tip

Annotate the text by underlining facts about exercise and writing comments in the margins about exercise increasing student attention and focus.

A Smart Move
by Jakob Tayler

Want to improve your test scores? It's time to hit the gym before you hit the books. Exercise can make you smarter.

Credulous? So were researchers themselves at first. But at least according to one German study, exercise improves attention and focus. There, high-school students completed a complex physical activity. Afterward, they scored higher on concentration tasks.

Dr. John Ratey, a Harvard Medical School professor, explains in his book *Spark*, "Exercise improves concentration, attention, motivation, and general overall mood, and decreases impulsivity." He thinks working out could help us with conditions such as ADHD and depression.

It's not just teens who benefit. A study out of Illinois looked at children. Incredibly, it found kids who exercise think more sharply and learn more quickly. Those who made fitness a regular part of their routine got higher scores on reasoning and memory tests.

Did you catch that part about "memory tests"? Sure enough, being active improves our memory, too. Irish researchers had a group of young men ride bikes before a memory test. Another group didn't cycle. Give yourself a hand if you guessed the bike-riders remembered better. After, tests showed an increase in a protein in the blood. That protein supports and promotes the growth of neurons. In other words, exercise helps us nourish and grow new brain cells.

And it seems it's never too late to start. Another study focused on overweight, inactive adults. After four months of recurring exercise, two things happened. First, they lost weight. Second, their mental acuity improved, which is a fancy way of saying they began thinking more clearly. A number of studies on the elderly concur with similar results.

As Dr. Ratey himself explains: "Nothing we know of—no drugs, no activity—nothing else competes with what physical exercise does to increase the number of new brain cells that we make every day."

But don't just take my word for it. Try it yourself!

page 1

"A Smart Move" *(cont.)*

Directions

1. Read the writing prompt.

2. If directed by your teacher, find one additional, credible source related to your topic.

3. Take notes below to organize your notes on ways exercise helps students focus.

4. Argue the prompt given with your own words by drawing evidence from texts to support analysis/reflection and including the facts in your answer. Include facts from your sources.

5. Include textual evidence (quotations or paraphrasing) and at least two in-text citations. Create a bibliography, and include it at the end of your writing.

> Writing should be organized in the following way:
>
> - an **introduction** that previews the topic and states a clear claim
> - a **body of content** with relevant evidence and textual citations
> - a **conclusion** that summarizes and supports the claim

Writing Prompt 3

Use details from the text to explain two ways exercise can help students academically.

How exercise helps students

Cause-and-Effect Text Structure

✎ Materials

- copies of *"Win or Lose?"* (pages 100–101; page100.pdf)

Procedure

1. Distribute *"Win or Lose?"* (pages 100–101). Have students read the prompt related to the passage. The prompt is: *Using examples from the text, support the idea that winning the lottery might not always be positive.*

2. Have students read the text independently and think about how they will need to respond to the prompt.

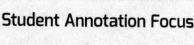

Student Annotation Focus

While each student reads, have them underline and number the facts indicating ways in which winning the lottery might not be a positive thing.

3. Assign the writing prompt on page 101.

4. Have students use the information from the text to respond to the prompt. You may choose to allow each student to use one additional credible source.

5. Remind students to follow the directions and to use textual evidence and citations. Remind students that a citation is needed directly following a quotation. In this case, the abbreviation *par.* is used to reference a specific paragraph.

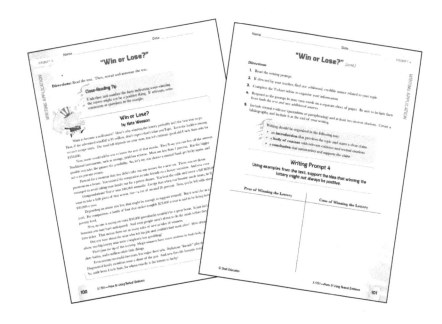

"Win or Lose?"

Directions: Read the text. Then, reread and annotate the text.

Close-Reading Tip

Underline and number the facts indicating ways winning the lottery might not be a positive thing. If relevant, write comments or questions in the margin.

Win or Lose?
by Kete Wesson

Want to become a millionaire? Here's why winning the lottery probably isn't the best way to go. First, if the advertised windfall is $1 million, don't expect that's what you'll get. Even the luckiest among us can't escape taxes. The total bill depends on your state, but let's estimate good old Uncle Sam asks for $350,000.

Now, many would advise you to invest the rest of that moola. They'll say you can live off the interest. Traditional investments, such as savings, yield low returns. Most are less than 1 percent. But the bigger gamble you take, the greater the possibility. So, let's say you choose a mutual fund, get lucky again, and net a six percent return.

Pretend for a moment that you didn't take out any money for a new car. There was no down payment on a house. You resisted the temptation to take friends on a luxury vacation. And you even managed to avoid taking your family out for a pricey dinner. You beat the odds and invest a full $650,000.

Congratulations! You've won $40,000 annually. Except that when our favorite uncle hears, he'll want to take a little piece of that action, too—a cut of around 26 percent. Now, you're left with about $30,000 a year.

Depending on where you live, that might be enough to support yourself. But it won't be at a high level. For comparison, a family of four that makes roughly $23,000 a year is said to be living below the poverty level.

Now, no one is saying an extra $30,000 greenbacks wouldn't be a great boon. It just isn't the big bonanza you may have anticipated. And most people aren't about to do the math before they cash in that lotto ticket. That means there are as many tales of woe as tales of winners.

Did you hear about the man who left his job and couldn't find work after? How about the woman whose two big lottery wins were completely lost gambling?

That's just the tip of the iceberg. Mega-winners have come undone by bad deals, sour investments, dirty habits, and a million other little things.

Even among successful investors, few enjoy their win. Nefarious "friends" plot their murder. Disgruntled family members want a share of the pot. And new foes file lawsuits to take a piece of the pie. So, aside from Uncle Sam, for whom exactly is the lottery so lucky?

"Win or Lose?" *(cont.)*

Directions

1. Read the writing prompt.

2. If directed by your teacher, find one additional, credible source related to your topic.

3. Complete the T-chart below to organize your information.

4. Respond to the prompt in your own words on a separate sheet of paper. Be sure to include facts from both the text and any additional sources.

5. Include textual evidence (quotations or paraphrasing) and at least two in-text citations. Create a bibliography, and include it at the end of your writing.

Writing should be organized in the following way:

- an **introduction** that previews the topic and states a clear claim
- a **body of content** with relevant evidence and textual citations
- a **conclusion** that summarizes and supports the claim

Writing Prompt 4

Using examples from the text, support the idea that winning the lottery might not always be positive.

Pros of Winning the Lottery	Cons of Winning the Lottery

Sequence Text Structure

✏ Materials

- copies of *"Cracking the Color Wheel"* (pages 103–104; page103.pdf)

Procedure

1. Distribute *"Cracking the Color Wheel"* (pages 103–104). Have students read the prompt related to the passage. The prompt is: *Explain how the author uses ratios and percentages to prove the color blue's popularity. Use the text to support your answer.*

2. Have students read the text independently and think about how they will respond to the prompt.

Student Annotation Focus

While students read, have them underline statistics that could help with their responses to the prompt. If relevant, have them write comments in the margins.

3. Assign the writing prompt on page 104.

4. Have students use the information from the text to respond to the prompt. You may choose to allow each student to use one additional credible source.

5. Remind students to follow the directions and to use textual evidence and citations.

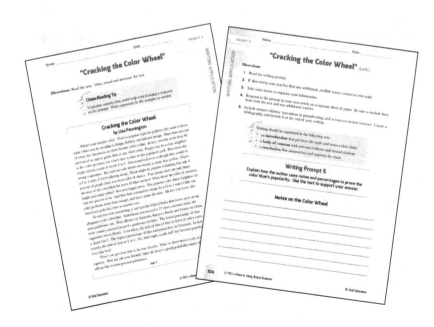

"Cracking the Color Wheel"

Directions: Read the text. Then, reread and annotate the text.

Close-Reading Tip

Underline statistics that could help with forming a response to the prompt. Write comments in the margins as needed.

Cracking the Color Wheel
by Lisa Pennington

What's your favorite color? That's a popular topic for pollsters who want to know what colors may be trending in design, fashion, and interior design. More than two out of every five Americans say their favorite color is blue. In fact, recently, more than 40 percent of us said we prefer blue to any other color. Purple may be a close neighbor in the color spectrum, but it isn't close to blue in this popularity poll. Blue beats this royal color by a ratio of nearly 2 to 1. Green and red seem as though they would be strong contenders. But each has only about one-fourth as many fans as blue. (That's a 4 to 1 ratio, if you're playing along.) Black might be popular in fashion, but only 6 percent of people claim it as their color of choice. That means there are only three devotees of the color black for every 20 blue backers! What about the color of summer, bright and sunny yellow? Not such happy news. This primary color shines brightest for only five percent of us. And blue fans outnumber orange by a 10 to 1 ratio! Only one color performs worse than orange, and that's plain old white. Merely 1 in every 100 Americans picks this color as number one.

In case you were wondering, it isn't just the United States that shows such strong allegiance to the color blue. Individuals interviewed in 17 other countries share the same preference, too. From Mexico to Australia, Korea to Brazil, and France to China, every country surveyed showed a preference for blue. The lowest percentage of blue supporters was in Russia. Even there, the ratio of fans of blue to those of other colors is about 3 to 7. The highest percentage of blue enthusiasts lives in Germany. In that country, the ratio is close to 1 to 1. Yes, that's right, nearly half the German populace loves blue best!

There's no question blue is the true favorite. What we don't know is why it reigns supreme. Why not ask your friends? After all, there's a good probability many of them will say blue is their personal preference.

page 1

"Cracking the Color Wheel" *(cont.)*

Directions

1. Read the writing prompt.

2. If directed by your teacher, find one additional, credible source related to your topic.

3. Take notes below to organize your information.

4. Respond to the prompt in your own words on a separate sheet of paper. Be sure to include facts from both the text and any additional sources.

5. Include textual evidence (quotations or paraphrasing) and at least two in-text citations. Create a bibliography, and include it at the end of your writing.

Writing should be organized in the following way:

- an **introduction** that previews the topic and states a clear claim
- a **body of content** with relevant evidence and textual citations
- a **conclusion** that summarizes and supports the claim

Writing Prompt 5

Explain how the author uses ratios and percentages to prove the color blue's popularity. Use the text to support your answer.

Notes on the Color Wheel

_____

_____

_____

_____

_____

_____

Description Text Structure

✎ Materials

- copies of *"Peanuts—A Potential Hazard"* (pages 106–107; page106.pdf)

Procedure

1. Distribute *"Peanuts—A Potential Hazard"* (pages 106–107). Have students read the prompt related to the passage. The prompt is: *Using the text as support, describe how peanut allergies can affect people and what occurs during an allergic reaction.*

2. Have students read the text independently and think about how they will respond to the prompt.

Student Annotation Focus

While students read, have them circle the information that explains peanut allergies and underline any information that is about allergic reactions. If relevant, write comments in the margin.

3. Assign the writing prompt on page 107.

4. Have students use the information from the text to respond to the prompt. You may choose to allow each student to use one additional credible source.

5. Remind students to follow the directions and to use textual evidence and citations.

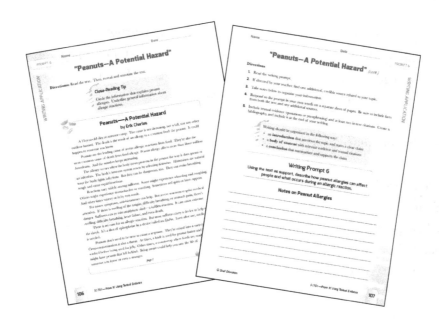

WRITING APPLICATION

"Peanuts—A Potential Hazard"

Directions: Read the text. Then, reread and annotate the text.

> ### Close-Reading Tip
>
> Circle the information that explains peanut allergies. Underline general information about allergic reactions.

Peanuts——A Potential Hazard
by Erik Charles

A 13-year-old dies at summer camp. The cause is not drowning, nor a fall, nor any other outdoor hazard. The death is the result of an allergy to a common food: the peanut. It could happen to someone you know.

Peanuts are the leading cause of severe allergic reactions from food. They're also the most common cause of death from food allergy. Peanut allergy affects more than three million Americans. And the number keeps increasing.

The allergy occurs when the body views proteins in the peanut the way it does germs or an infection. The body's immune system reacts by releasing *histamines*. Histamines are natural ways the body fights infections. But they can be dangerous, too. They can make breathing tough and cause rapid heartbeat.

Reactions vary widely among sufferers. Some might experience wheezing and coughing. Others might experience stomachaches or vomiting. Sometimes red spots or hives appear. And other times watery or itchy eyes result.

For minor symptoms, anti-histamines can help. But severe reactions require medical attention. If there is swelling of the tongue, difficulty breathing, or stomach pain, there's danger. Sufferers can go into *anaphylactic shock*—a sudden reaction. It can cause extreme swelling, difficulty breathing, heart failure, and even death.

There is no cure for an allergic reaction. But most sufferers carry a device to help treat the shock. It's a shot of epinephrine in a device called an *EpiPen*. Even after use, medical help is needed.

Peanuts don't need to be near to cause a response. They're mixed into a variety of foods. Cross-contamination is also a threat. At times, a knife is used for peanut butter and isn't washed before being used for jelly. Other times, a countertop where foods are made might have peanut dust left behind. Being aware could help you save the life of someone you know or even a stranger.

page 1

"Peanuts—A Potential Hazard" *(cont.)*

Directions

1. Read the writing prompt.

2. If directed by your teacher, find one additional, credible source related to your topic.

3. Take notes below to organize your information.

4. Respond to the prompt in your own words on a separate sheet of paper. Be sure to include facts from both the text and any additional sources.

5. Include textual evidence (quotations or paraphrasing) and at least two in-text citations. Create a bibliography, and include it at the end of your writing.

Writing should be organized in the following way:

- an **introduction** that previews the topic and states a clear claim
- a **body of content** with relevant evidence and textual citations
- a **conclusion** that summarizes and supports the claim

Writing Prompt 6

Using the text as support, describe how peanut allergies can affect people and what occurs during an allergic reaction.

Notes on Peanut Allergies

_____

_____

_____

_____

_____

_____

_____

WRITING APPLICATION

Description Text Structure

✏ Materials

- copies of *"Racing Rocks"*
  (pages 109–110;
  page109.pdf)

Procedure

1. Distribute *"Racing Rocks"* (pages 109–110). Have students read the prompt related to the passage. The prompt is: *Summarize the central idea of the text, and identify the specific details that support this idea.*

2. Have students read the text independently and think about how they will need to answer the prompt.

Student Annotation Focus

While students read, have them identify and circle the main idea. Additionally, have students underline which key details are essential to understanding the main idea.

3. Assign the writing prompt on page 110.

4. Have students use the information from the text to respond to the prompt. You may choose to allow each student to use one additional credible source.

5. Remind students to follow the directions and to use textual evidence and citations. Remind students that a citation is needed directly following a quotation. In this case, the abbreviation *par.* is used to reference a specific paragraph.

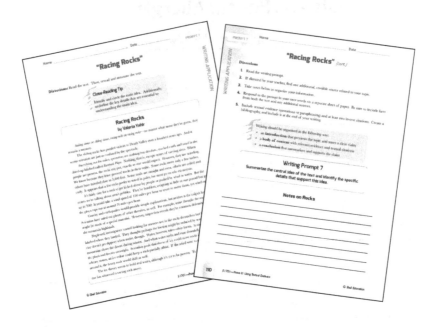

Name _____ Date _____

"Racing Rocks"

Directions: Read the text. Then, reread and annotate the text.

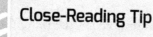

Close-Reading Tip

Identify and circle the main idea. Additionally, underline the key details that are essential to understanding the main idea.

Racing Rocks
by Valeria Yahir

Sailing stones or *sliding stones, roving rocks* or *racing rocks*—no matter what name they're given, they remain a mystery.

The sliding rocks first puzzled visitors to Death Valley over a hundred years ago. And it seems scientists are just as confused by the spectacle.

Stretching out for miles, spectators see nothing but desolate, cracked earth and sand in the dried-up lakebed called *Racetrack Playa*. Nothing, that is, except stones of varying sizes. When people are present, the rocks stay put, exactly as one would expect. However, they are traveling. We know because they leave grooved tracks in their wake. Some rocks move only a few inches, others have traveled close to 3,000 feet. Some trails are straight and even, others are coiled and curly. It appears that a few rocks prefer to travel in pairs, but most go on solo excursions.

It's fairly easy for a rock to get kicked about by people or pushed by wind or water. But the stones we're talking about aren't pebbles. They're boulders, weighing as little as one pound but go up to 700! It would take a wind speed of 150 miles per hour or more to move them, yet wind on the playa tops out at around 70 miles per hour.

Gravity and earthquakes would provide simple explanations, but neither is the culprit here. Scientists have ruled out plenty of other theories, as well. For example, some thought the rocks might be made of a special material. However, inspection reveals they're common dolomite from the mountain highlands.

Perplexed, investigators started looking for answers not in the rocks themselves but in the dry lakebed where they landed. They thought perhaps the friction might be reduced by water. The clay doesn't get slippery when moist, though. Water, however, takes other forms. It snows in the mountains above the desert during winter. And when water melts and runs downhill, it collects in the playa and freezes overnight. Scientists posit that sheets of ice could move rocks in pairs. For solitary stones, an ice collar could keep a rock partially afloat. If the wind were to move the water around it, the heavy rock would shift as well.

The ice theory seems to hold real water, although it's yet to be proven. To this day, still no one has witnessed a racing rock move.

"Racing Rocks" *(cont.)*

Directions

1. Read the writing prompt.

2. If directed by your teacher, find one additional, credible source related to your topic.

3. Take notes below to organize your information.

4. Respond to the prompt in your own words on a separate sheet of paper. Be sure to include facts from both the text and any additional sources.

5. Include textual evidence (quotations or paraphrasing) and at least two in-text citations. Create a bibliography, and include it at the end of your writing.

Writing should be organized in the following way:

- an **introduction** that previews the topic and states a clear claim
- a **body of content** with relevant evidence and textual citations
- a **conclusion** that summarizes and supports the claim

Writing Prompt 7

Summarize the central idea of the text and identify the specific details that support this idea.

Notes on Rocks

_____

_____

_____

_____

_____

_____

Classification Text Structure

✏️ Materials

- copies of *"Super-Tasters"* (pages 112–113; page112.pdf)
- highlighters

Procedure

1. Distribute *"Super-Tasters"* (pages 112–113). Have students read the prompt related to the passage. The prompt is: *Classify super-tasters, non-tasters, and those in between by defining each term. Include the benefits of being a super-taster. Use the text to support your answer.*

2. Have students read the text independently and think about how they will answer the prompt.

Student Annotation Focus

While each student reads, have them put a number next to information relating to each type of taster (i.e., *1: super-taster*). Then, have students highlight the information vital to each category, using a different colored highlighter for each category.

3. Assign the writing prompt on page 113.

4. Have students use the information from the text to respond to the prompt. You may choose to allow each student to use one additional credible source.

5. Remind students to follow the directions and to use textual evidence and citations.

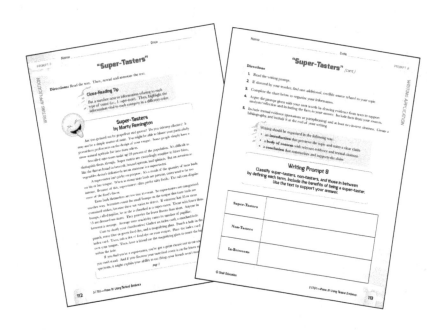

Name _____ Date _____

"Super-Tasters"

Directions: Read the text. Then, reread and annotate the text.

Close-Reading Tip

Put a number next to information relating to each type of taster (i.e., *1: super-taster*). Then, highlight the information vital to each category in a different color.

Super-Tasters
by Marty Remington

Are you grossed out by grapefruit and greens? Do you sidestep cilantro? It may not be a simple matter of taste. You might be able to blame your particularly persnickety preferences on the design of your tongue. Some people simply have a more natural aptitude for taste than others.

So-called *super-tasters* make up 25 percent of the population. It's difficult to distinguish them, though. Super tasters are exceedingly sensitive to bitter bites, like the flavors found in broccoli, brussel sprouts, and spinach. But an aversion to vegetables doesn't definitively mean someone is a super-taster.

A super-taster isn't picky on purpose. It's a result of the quantity of taste buds on his or her tongue. When so many taste buds are present, tastes tend to be too intense. Because of this, super-tasters often prefer salty foods. The salt can disguise some of the food's flavor.

Taste buds themselves are too tiny to count. So super-tasters are categorized another way. Scientists count the small bumps on the tongue that taste buds are contained within, because these are easier to detect. If someone has 35 or more bumps, called *papillae*, he or she is classified as a super-taster. Those with fewer than 15 are deemed *non-tasters*. They perceive far fewer flavors than most. Anyone in between is average. Average taste sensitivity varies by number of papillae.

Care to clarify your classification? Gather an index card, a standard hole punch, some blue or green food dye, and a magnifying glass. Punch a hole in the index card. Then, rub a dot of food dye on your tongue. Place the index card over your tongue. Then, have a friend use the magnifying glass to count the bumps within the hole.

If you find you're a super-taster, you've got a great excuse not to eat something you can't stand. And if you discover your taste-bud count is on the lower end of the spectrum, it might explain your ability to eat things your friends won't touch.

page 1

"Super-Tasters" (cont.)

Directions

1. Read the writing prompt.

2. If directed by your teacher, find one additional, credible source related to your topic.

3. Complete the chart below to organize your information.

4. Argue the prompt given with your own words by drawing evidence from texts to support analysis/reflection and including the facts in your answer. Include facts from your sources.

5. Include textual evidence (quotations or paraphrasing) and at least two in-text citations. Create a bibliography, and include it at the end of your writing.

> Writing should be organized in the following way:
> - an **introduction** that previews the topic and states a clear claim
> - a **body of content** with relevant evidence and textual citations
> - a **conclusion** that summarizes and supports the claim

Writing Prompt 8

Classify super-tasters, non-tasters, and those in between by defining each term. Include the benefits of being a super-taster. Use the text to support your answer.

Super-Tasters	
Non-Tasters	
In-Betweens	

WRITING APPLICATION

Problem-and-Solution Text Structure

✏️ Materials

- copies of *"Do You Hear What I Hear?"* (pages 115–116; page115.pdf)

Procedure

1. Distribute *"Do You Hear What I Hear?"* (pages 115–116). Have students read the prompt related to the passage. The prompt is: *Identify the problem that Howard Stapleton addressed and what he did to solve it. Use the text to support your answer.*

2. Have students read the text independently and think about how they will answer the prompt.

Student Annotation Focus

While students read, have them circle the problem and underline the solutions.

3. Assign the writing prompt on page 116.

4. Have students use the information from the text to respond to the prompt. You may choose to allow each student to use one additional credible source.

5. Remind students to follow the directions and to use textual evidence and citations.

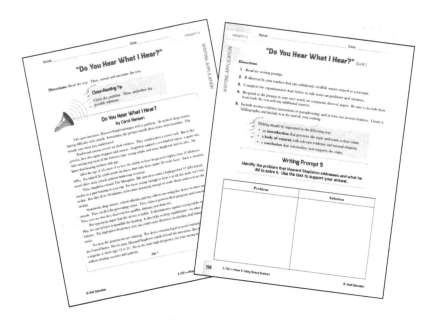

"Do You Hear What I Hear?"

Directions: Read the text. Then, reread and annotate the text.

Close-Reading Tip

Circle the problem. Then, underline the possible solutions.

Do You Hear What I Hear?
by Carol Hansen

Like most inventors, Howard Stapleton began with a problem. He noticed shop owners having difficulty with crowds. Sometimes, the groups outside their stores were harmless. The trouble was when they misbehaved.

Traditional alarms weren't an ideal solution. They could scatter a crowd well. But in the process, they also upset shoppers and owners. Stapleton wanted a new kind of alarm: a quiet one. After noting that most of the loiterers were young adults and teens, Stapleton had an idea. He knew that hearing declines with age.

After the age of 25, most of us lose the ability to hear frequencies higher than 15 kilohertz (kHz). So, what if he could create an alarm that only those under 25 could hear? Such a creation would drive away crowds without bothering everyone.

Thus, Stapleton created The Mosquito. His invention emits a high-pitched 17 kHz sound, similar to a gnat buzzing in your ear. For those young enough to hear it at all, the noise isn't bad at first. But after 20 to 30 minutes, it becomes annoying enough to make them want to leave the vicinity.

Worldwide, shop owners, school officials, and law officers are using the device to drive away crowds. They credit it for preventing crime. They claim it protects their property and customers. They even say that they deal with less graffiti, damage, and drug use.

But opponents argue that the device is unfair. It discriminates against young adults and teens. Plus, the ear isn't just responsible for hearing. It also helps us keep equilibrium—in other words, balance. The high-pitch frequency, they say, could cause dizziness, headaches, and nausea as a result.

For now, the proponents are winning. The device remains legal in most countries, including the United States. For his part, Howard Stapleton stands behind his invention. But he also markets a ringtone to those ages 12 to 25. Set at the same high frequency, the tone means teens can text without alerting teachers and parents.

page 1

WRITING APPLICATION

"Do You Hear What I Hear?" *(cont.)*

Directions

1. Read the writing prompt.

2. If directed by your teacher, find one additional, credible source related to your topic.

3. Complete the organizational chart below to take notes on problems and solutions.

4. Respond to the prompt in your own words on a separate sheet of paper. Be sure to include facts from both the text and any additional sources.

5. Include textual evidence (quotations or paraphrasing) and at least two in-text citations. Create a bibliography, and include it at the end of your writing.

> Writing should be organized in the following way:
>
> *   an **introduction** that previews the topic and states a clear claim
> *   a **body of content** with relevant evidence and textual citations
> *   a **conclusion** that summarizes and supports the claim

Writing Prompt 9

Identify the problem that Howard Stapleton addresses and what he did to solve it. Use the text to support your answer.

Problem	Solution

© *Shell Education*

Compare-and-Contrast Text Structure

Materials

- copies of *"A Royal Pastime"* (pages 118–119; page118.pdf)
- highlighters

Procedure

1. Distribute *"A Royal Pastime"* (pages 118–119). Have students read the prompt related to the passage. The prompt is: *Compare the fitness routines of Elisabeth, Diana, and Kate. Has exercise changed over time? Use the text to support your answer.*

2. Have students read the text independently and think about how they will answer the prompt.

Student Annotation Focus

While students read, have them annotate text related to the prompt. Have students highlight information relating to the exercise routines using different colored highlighters for each royal member.

3. Assign the writing prompt on page 119.

4. Have students use the information from the text to respond to the prompt. You may choose to allow each student to use one additional credible source.

5. Remind students to follow the directions and to use textual evidence and citations.

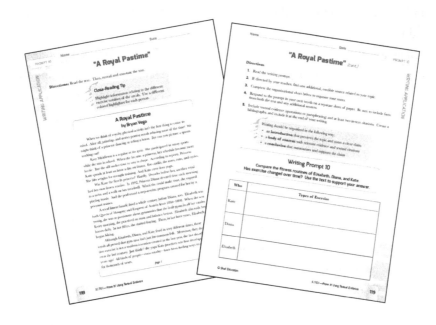

Name _____ Date _____

"A Royal Pastime"

Directions: Read the text. Then, reread and annotate the text.

Close-Reading Tip

Highlight information relating to the different exercise routines of the royals. Use a different colored highlighter for each person.

A Royal Pastime
by Bryan Vega

When we think of royalty, physical activity isn't the first thing to come to mind. After all, paintings and stories portray royals relaxing most of the time! We might think of a princess dancing or riding a horse. But can you picture a queen working out?

Kate Middleton is a regular at the gym. She participated in many sports while she was in school. When she became a princess, her schedule became more hectic. But she still makes time to stay in shape. According to reports, Princess Kate spends at least an hour a day on fitness. For cardio, she rows, runs, and cycles. She lifts weights for strength training. And Kate even does yoga.

Was Kate the first fit princess? Hardly. Decades before her, another royal had her own fitness routine. In 1992, Princess Diana devoted time each morning to a swim and a walk on her treadmill. When she could make time, she enjoyed playing tennis. And she performed a step-aerobic program created for her by a personal trainer.

A royal fitness fanatic lived a whole century before Diana, too. Elisabeth was both Queen of Hungary and Empress of Austria from 1884–1898. When she was young, she was so passionate about gymnastics that she built gyms in all her castles. Every morning, she practiced on mats and balance beams. Elisabeth also rode her horses daily. In her fifties, she started fencing. Then, in her later years, Elisabeth began hiking.

Although Elisabeth, Diana, and Kate lived in very different times, these royals all proved that gym time isn't just for common folk. Moreover, they show that exercise is not a modern invention created in the last year, the last decade, or even the last century. Just think—the yoga Kate practices was first developed 5,000 years ago! All kinds of people—even royalty—have been finding ways to stay fit for thousands of years.

page 1

"A Royal Pastime" *(cont.)*

Directions

1. Read the writing prompt.

2. If directed by your teacher, find one additional, credible source related to your topic.

3. Complete the organizational chart below to organize your notes.

4. Respond to the prompt in your own words on a separate sheet of paper. Be sure to include facts from both the text and any additional sources.

5. Include textual evidence (quotations or paraphrasing) and at least two in-text citations. Create a bibliography, and include it at the end of your writing.

Writing should be organized in the following way:

- an **introduction** that previews the topic and states a clear claim
- a **body of content** with relevant evidence and textual citations
- a **conclusion** that summarizes and supports the claim

Writing Prompt 10

Compare the fitness routines of Elisabeth, Diana, and Kate.
Has exercise changed over time? Use the text to support your answer.

Who	Types of Exercise
Kate	
Diana	
Elisabeth	

Appendices

Answer Key

There are many open-ended questions and writing prompts in this book. For those activities, the answers provided here are examples.

Textual Evidence in Reading

Lesson 1

Matching (page 17)

1. D; 2. A; 3. E; 4. C; 5. B

True/False (page 19)

1. True; 2. False; 3. False; 4. True; 5. True.

Lesson 2

"Namesake" (page 22)

1. Alex seems to dislike that she was named after a male baseball player because she says "never mind that I'm a girl" (Button 1).

2. Jackie Mitchell was a successful baseball player because she strikes out Babe Ruth and "does the same thing with Lou Gehrig" (Button 1).

"A Long Lost Hero" (page 23)

1. Drummer boys helped injured soldiers by carrying "the injured away from the battlefield on stretchers" (Hall 1).

2. Drummers also "drummed communications on the battlefield when it was too loud to hear shouts" (Hall 1).

Lesson 3

"Lost in Translation" (page 25)

1. Nature came alive to the author in many ways. For example, trees are personified in a way to show that they are calling to him:

   The trees called me to visit Zion National Park. These trees have difficult lives, enduring high temperatures with little water to quench their thirst. They make their homes along high cliffs as they plant their roots in inhospitable rock. Yet despite the odds, twisting junipers and squat piñons, towering aspens and welcoming cottonwoods survive and even thrive (Blaine 1).

"Up Close and Personal" (page 26)

1. Bernadette explains that she got different genes from her parents. She does this by saying,

   "I know this one. I'm an AG. I can drink milk, but my mom can't. That makes the G from her and the A from my dad." It was pretty cool to see her parents' influence. She knew from her analysis that she had large pieces of DNA identical to her siblings and almost as many common portions with her cousins (Brinkley 1).

Lesson 4

"Khufu's Tomb" (page 28)

1. The secret of Mao is apparent as the story unfolds. The author gives us clues such as Mao having night vision, the act of her trotting and circling the king's legs, and she never speaks which are all things not common to a human beings. However, the ending really gives it away when the author references Mao's paws. This solidifies that Mao must be a cat (Williams 1).

2. You can tell Mao and the king have a close relationship because she "laid her head on Khufu's shoulder as he stroked her back" (Williams 1). That shows a sort of intimacy that people typically only share with one they feel close to.

"The Dragon Jewel" (page 29)

1. At the beginning of the story, the prince is a "great boaster" (Kellog 1) and is not afraid of the dragon. By the end, the prince becomes frightened.

2. Prince Lofty is afraid the storm will kill everyone, and he clings to the boat "begging the servants to save him" (Kellog 1).

Answer Key (cont.)

Lesson 5

"Fall Leaves Fall" (page 31)

1. For example, point out that one part of the text mentions that, "Every leaf speaks bliss to me" (Bronte 3). Later, the text states, "I shall smile when the wreaths of snow / Blossom where the rose should grow" (Bronte 7–8).

"Young and Old" (page 32)

1. The author feels sad about getting older. You can tell because Kingsley uses sad language such as "stale" (11) and "maimed" (14) to describe getting older.

Reading Application Practice

Author's Purpose—"Mars Mission Application" (page 35)

1. In *Mars Mission Application*, Al Aboutmee sends an email to the Mars selection committee trying to persuade them to consider him as a candidate. In the beginning of the email, he uses persuasion by explaining that he can handle the training program, he is resourceful, and that he is, "… willing to cut ties to be a part of this production" (Aboutmee par. 3). This email is not an official job application, but it is written to represent one.

2. The beginning of the application focuses on skills Al has that would be beneficial to the program. He then proceeds to asks several thoughtless questions that shows him to be self-serving. One question is about gardening; he goes on to say, "planting and tending vegetables is not really my thing" (Aboutmee par. 7). These types of questions are inappropriate for a job application.

3. The author wrote this email because his audience is young kids who tend to become bored if the writing is too formal. Asking to bring his dog because, "…animals have a high audience appeal" (Aboutmee par. 8) is the type of silliness that makes this email appealing. If this job application was written to be read by college students, its content would be written at a higher reading level.

Text Structure—"DIY: Homemade Fireworks" (page 40)

1. This is informational and appears to be geared towards kids. The author tells the reader to "follow these simple steps" (Tayler par. 1), which tells that the text is informational. Throughout the text, the author gives specific instructions for the reader to follow to make "fireworks" on their own.

2. The author is using sequence text structure by giving steps to follow in a certain order. If Tayler wrote, "Open your hand so all the candies fall into the bottle" (Tayler par. 4), at the beginning of the directions, you would not be able to create fireworks correctly. These directions need to be followed the way the author intended.

3. In the beginning of the text, it says, "if you're ready for some loud blasts and complete mayhem" (Tayler par. 1). This is a good indicator that the author is going to try to relate to kids by using humor. DIY guides tend to be dry and to the point, but this author uses phrases such as, "Just kidding" and "claim the glory that's rightfully yours" to hold on to the reader's attention.

Main Idea—Excerpt from "Dr. Martin Luther King Jr." (page 44)

1. The main idea of this story focuses on how Dr. Martin Luther King Jr. struggled to achieve equality among all people. He felt he had to get "the nation's attention focused on the civil rights problem (Jefe par. 6) by using peaceful protests. What Dr. King did was bring attention to segregation in the South without violence, eventually giving African Americans more rights.

2. "A Letter from Jail" is about Dr. King's time spent in jail for participating and encouraging civil rights protest. Once in jail, he realized he needed to continue to be heard, so he wrote a letter to his followers stating, "the only way to spur change was to bring attention to it and protesting accomplishes this" (Jefe par. 5). King used freedom of speech in a peaceful way, to gain attention to the injustice of the South.

3. Project C was a plan Dr. King used to confront (C) the owners of department stores. Instead

of buying new clothes, he "showed up in old clothes because…he would rather wear old work clothes" (Jefe par. 2). This came about because stores would allow African Americans to buy merchandise, but they were not allowed to use the restrooms or eat in their stores.

Identifying Literary Devices—"Race the Wind" (page 48)

1. The author uses figurative language throughout the text to paint a picture for the reader. The "sand kicking up and lashing our faces" (Aaron par. 1) at the beginning of the story, makes the reader wonder what is happening. The wind was referred to as "screaming" twice in the story, indicating that the storm was loud. It is very easy to visualize this story, due to the figurative language used.

2. The sentence, "The spout sprinted over the final stretch of water, an animal eager to make the kill" (Aaron par. 6), uses two types of literary devices. The "spout sprinting" is personification because the spout is given human characteristics and refers to how fast the spout was moving. The sentence is also a metaphor because it compares the spout to an animal making a kill.

3. Figurative language is used throughout "Race the Wind" to help the reader's understanding of the intensity of the storm. The sky is described as a "dark wall of clouds marched toward us" (Aaron par. 2), and the waterspout is called the "liquid sister of the tornado" (Aaron par. 4). Integrating figurative language into a story, gives the reader a better visual image and makes the text more interesting.

Compare and Contrast—"The Golden Age—from *Old Greek Stories*" (page 52)

1. In the story, "The Golden Age," Saturn is described as a Titan that is very old, whereas, Jupiter is his son and much younger. Under Saturn's reign, "Men were never so happy" (Baldwin par. 2), while Jupiter's reign brought violence to the Earth and "men grew dissatisfied" (Baldwin par. 8). Even though the two gods were father and son, they were as different as night and day.

2. In paragraph 8, the men became greedy, selfish, and unkind. "Some wanted to be rich, owning all the best things in the world" (Baldwin par. 8) describes the past, but is very similar to our world today. So many people in today's world, only care about having possessions, money and power, not unlike those referred to under Jupiter's rule.

3. The Golden Age was almost paradise-like, "Springtime lasted all year" (Baldwin par. 2), and food was abundant. Everybody had money, friends, and didn't have to work. Life was good during this time period.

Synthesizing and Summarizing—Excerpt from "The Bread Book" (page 56)

1. Some information in Excerpt from "The Bread Book" is there to give the reader fun facts that are not necessary to the article but can be amusing tidbits to know. It is interesting to know that people used to use "stones to grind wheat into flour" (Martin 1).

2. Excerpt from "The Bread Book" is about how it "has historically been one the world's most important and convenient foods" (Martin 1). The passage focuses on the process of making a loaf of bread, from the farm to the consumer.

3. A loaf of bread starts out as grains of wheat (kernels) cultivated by the farmer. Next, "the kernels are sent to flour mills where the milling turns the kernels into flour" (Martin 1). Once it is flour, the bakers use it to make loaves of bread.

Making Inferences—"Waiting and Watching" (page 60)

1. After reading the passage, I have concluded that the narrator must be from another world. In the first paragraph, the narrator refers to people on Earth as "creatures" they would like to communicate with. After describing the growth of civilization with the Mayas, the passage states, "many hundreds of years from now, the Earth may be populated with a civilization we can approach" (Victor par. 7). If the narrator was from another country, he would not keep mentioning the planet Earth throughout the story and his desire to wait until the Earth is more advanced.

Answer Key (cont.)

2. In the story "Waiting and Watching," the narrator wants to communicate with people of the Earth but shows he is a patient being who will, "continue to watch and wait" (Victor par. 7). The narrator, and those he is with, must be intellectuals and far more advanced than the civilization of the Mayas, if they do not want to approach them and will wait.

3. The narrator describes the Mayas as the first community that has given them any hope of communicating with people. The Mayas' understanding of math and recognizing "that a year contains 365 days on Earth" (Victor, par. 4) indicate to the ones that are watching that people are starting to show promise of becoming an intelligent species.

Identifying Key Details—Excerpt from "Sound Waves and Communication"
(page 64)

1. Wavelengths can be used to measure sound. The text describes wavelength as the distance between the two peaks of the same wave" (Shrill par. 1). Wavelengths are also related to the frequency and pitch of a sound.

2. The definition of frequency is, "how many times a particle vibrates in a second." (Shrill par. 1). Frequency uses sound waves to create the pitch of a sound. "Short wavelengths create high frequencies and sound shrill in pitch" (Shrill par. 2), while long wavelengths are the opposite in sound—a deep pitch.

3. The Doppler effect refers to the pitch. The example given in the article refers to sirens and as they "approach, the sound seems very shrill, but after they pass, the pitch seems to grow deeper" (Shrill par. 3). Another example would be an airplane flying by; the pitch drops lower after it passes.

Asking Questions—"Tell Me Again, Dad"
(page 68)

1. The narrator loved listening to stories his daddy told him about his granddaddy. The stories refer to Granddaddy's life as a hobo during the Great Depression and due to the lack of jobs, "they took to the railroads, looking for work, money, and food…" (Wayne 1). The narrator wondering if his granddaddy's talent was storytelling was probably because of the stories he had already heard.

2. In the story, "Tell Me Again, Dad", the term *hobo* referred to men who traveled to work and "carried farming tools with them, so people called them "hoe boys" or "hobos" for short" (Wayne 1). The name may have become insulting over the years, but in the beginning, men were just trying to find a respectable job that would take care of their needs. There is nothing derogatory about being a hard-working man.

3. In the reading passage, the word *bartered* is used to describe how the workers traded a skill or item for something they may have needed. A context clue that helps with understanding the word is, "Some guys might sing for a cup of coffee" (Wayne 1). Bartering helped people when lack of money was a problem.

Compare and Contrast—"The Nutrient Cycle" (page 72)

1. Nitrogen and carbon are important to every living thing on Earth. They are both gases that play a big part in plant life, and therefore, our lives. When plants and animals die, "decomposers break down dead animals and allow the nutrients in their bodies" (Nye par. 4) and then the nitrogen and carbon cycle recycle into the soil and start over. Nitrogen and carbon are different because carbon uses carbon dioxide to help in the cell growth of every living thing, whereas nitrogen can only be in a certain form in order to help life.

2. Carbon uses photosynthesis to help with absorption of carbon dioxide into the plant's leaves. When an animal eats the plants, they "…use carbon to build and repair cells in their bodies" (Nye, par. 7). Nitrogen is a component of a plant's chlorophyll. Using solar energy, nitrogen "combine water and carbon dioxide to make sugar and oxygen" (Nye, par. 3). In other words, nitrogen is reliant on carbon and if there is not enough nitrogen, plants may die.

3. All living things on Earth are dependent on the nutrient cycle. Without green plants to help with cycling through sugar and oxygen, life would start to die off. Nitrogen makes up "78 percent of the atmosphere" (Nye par. 1) and "Carbon is found in every living thing on Earth" (Nye, par. 5). Humans would not be able to continue living without the help of the nutrient cycle.

Textual Evidence in Writing

Lesson 6

Using Credible and Reliable Sources Practice 1 (page 76)

1.a hard copy source such as a printed book; 2. a source available in digital format, not printed; 3. source that has to do with the topic; 4. source that can be trusted; 5. adopting a llama; 6. slime recipe; 7. how to get a passport; 8. YES; 9. NO; 10. NO; 11. NO; 12. YES

Using Credible and Reliable Sources Practice 2 (page 77)

1. countries involved with WWII; 2. homemade facial mask; 3. strangest mammals in the United States; 4. filtering photo apps; 5. largest mountains; 6; YES; 7. YES; 8. YES

Lesson 7

Supporting a Claim Practice 1 (page 79)

1. N; 2. RE; 3. LR; 4. RE; 5. RE; 6. RE; 7. LR

Supporting a Claim Practice 2 (page 80)

1. LR; 2. N; 3. RE; 4. RE; 5. LR; 6. RE; 7. LR; 8. RE

Lesson 10

Creating a Bibliography Practice 1
(page 88)

1. Player, Steve. *The Best Hobbies of the 21st Century*. Crater Publishing.

2. Flyer, Julie. *"Hobbies You Can Do."* Outdoor Adventure Magazine.

3. Hiker, Barb. *"Exploring the World Through Hobbies."* Hobbies. www.hobbies.com.

Creating a Bibliography Practice 2
(page 89)

1. Cruster, Hugh. Pizza from the Source: How Italians Do It. Clement Publishing.

2. Clinger, Jose. "Best Pizza Recipes in Mexico." Chef at Home Magazine.

3. Trail, Vivian. "Pizza Around the Globe." Recipes from Earth. www.recipesfromearth.com.

Text Evidence Vocabulary

Word/Phrase	Definition
cite	to quote from text to help support or prove a point
credible sources	sources the reader can trust and believe because they are authored or published by a reputable person or organization that uses research as evidence
direct quotation	the exact words of someone else woven into your writing, noted by using quotation marks
in-text citation	stating the author and page or paragraph number from a source when using a direct quotation
logical reasoning	statements that are written by the author that prove their claim makes sense
paraphrasing	restatement or rewording of an idea from a text
plagiarism	the practice of taking someone else's work and passing it off as your own
preferred style	a specialized way of ordering punctuation, grammar, and in-text citations from a specific set of guidelines
relevant evidence	facts that come from sources
relevant/reliable sources	sources that relate to the topic of a piece of writing
source	a place where information on a topic is gathered
text	the original piece of writing being cited
textual evidence	using evidence from a text to help with proving an argument, point, or fact

Direct Quotations
Text Evidence Starters

✏️ **The author states...**

✏️ **The author tells us that...**

✏️ **According to the text...**

✏️ **In paragraph _____, it says...**

✏️ **For instance, the text states...**

✏️ **When the author states...**

✏️ **One example from the text is...**

Paraphrasing Text Evidence Starters

✏️ **Based on the text...**

✏️ **The author explains that...**

✏️ **When the author describes...**

✏️ **The author implies that...**

✏️ **From the reading, we can tell that...**

✏️ **For instance, the text explains that...**

✏️ **For example, the text describes...**

Close-Reading Annotations Rubric

	3 points Quality	2 points Developing	1 point Approaching
Quality/Comprehension	Annotations show a thorough analysis of the text. **Indicators** • higher-level questions • key vocabulary questioned or identified • inferential comments • displays depth of thinking • clear attention to close-reading lesson focus	Annotations show some analysis of the text. **Indicators** • basic questions, • key vocabulary questioned • some inferential thinking, but most comments are concrete • comments only occasionally show depth • attempts to attend to close-reading lesson focus	Annotations show little or no analysis of the text. **Indicators** • demonstrates little understanding of the text with unrelated comments • comments often restate text • comments are only concrete • little or no attempt at close-reading lesson focus
Quantity	7–10 annotations	4–6 annotations	0–3 annotations

Citing Textual Evidence in Writing Rubric

	3 points Quality	2 points Developing	1 point Approaching
State Claim	The claim is clearly stated and applicable to the topic.	The claim is stated but may be unclear.	The topic is stated, but the claim is unclear or missing.
Evidence	Evidence from sources accurately responds to and supports the claim through direct quotations or paraphrasing.	Evidence from sources stays on topic, but its origin is unclear.	Evidence is not included or is inaccurate or unsupportive of topic or claim.
Explanation of Claim	An analysis and explanation strongly connect to and support claim.	An explanation of the claim is provided with some analysis or support.	There is little to no attempt at explaining the claim.
In-Text Citation and Document Sources	Citations of evidence are correctly provided; when applicable, sources are accurately documented.	Citations of evidence are sometimes provided; when applicable, sources are listed but may not include information needed.	Citations of evidence are attempted but may be inaccurate; even when applicable, sources are not listed.
Research	Sources are highly relevant to the topic, and credible.	Sources are somewhat relevant to the topic, and somewhat credible.	Sources are missing or used but may not be relevant or credible.

MLA Citing Source Reference

Standard Format of Citing within a Sentence

Direct Quotation	Paraphrasing
Example using author with paragraph number: According to Smith, "Automobile accidents are the number one cause of deaths for teenagers ages 15–20" (par. 1). with page number: According to Smith, "Automobile accidents are the number one cause of deaths for teenagers ages 15–20" (1). **Example using name of article** with paragraph number: According to the article, "Teen Accident Statistics," "Automobile accidents are the number one cause of deaths for teenagers ages 15–20" (par. 1). with page number: According to the article, "Teen Accident Statistics," "Automobile accidents are the number one cause of deaths for teenagers ages 15–20" (1).	**Original Passage:** There was a time when most teens were counting down to their 16th birthday. Nothing was more important than getting that key to freedom: the coveted driver's license. Acquiring a driver's license was much more important a generation ago, but no more. Driving a car used to be "cool" and a status symbol, but times have changed, and having a car doesn't have the same appeal as it did then. ("Priorities Are Changing" par. 1) **Acceptable Paraphrase:** When reading the article, "Priorities Are Changing," it is clear to see that being a teen driver, and having a car are not as "cool" as they used to be.

Standard Format of Citing at the End of a Sentence

Direct Quotation	Paraphrasing
Example using author with paragraph number: "Automobile accidents are the number one cause of deaths for teenagers ages 15–20" (Smith par. 1). with page number: "Automobile accidents are the number one cause of deaths for teenagers ages 15–20" (Smith 1). **Example using name of article** with paragraph number: "Automobile accidents are the number one cause of deaths for teenagers ages 15–20" ("Teen Accident Statistics" par. 1). with page number: "Automobile accidents are the number one cause of deaths for teenagers ages 15–20" ("Teen Accident Statistics" 1).	**Original Passage:** There was a time when most teens were counting down to their 16th birthday. Nothing was more important than getting that key to freedom: the coveted driver's license. Acquiring a driver's license was much more important a generation ago, but no more. Driving a car used to be "cool" and a status symbol, but times have changed, and having a car doesn't have the same appeal as it did then (Smith par. 1). **Acceptable Paraphrase:** Teenagers today are in no hurry to get their driver's licenses. They have different priorities from teens of the past (Smith par. 1).

APA is the most commonly used style within social sciences.
MLA is the most commonly used style within humanities.

How to Cite Textual Evidence in Reading

- Accurately ANSWER the question.

- Provide EVIDENCE from the reading passage to SUPPORT your answer.

- Correctly CITE the answer with (author paragraph or page number).

- Write a final thought to CONNECT or further explain your answer using logical reasoning.

Steps to Cite Textual Evidence in Writing

1. State claim.

2. Explain claim.

3. Research relevant and credible sources.

4. Use textual evidence from sources by quoting or paraphrasing.

5. Use in-text citations and document sources.

6. Connect or support your claim and evidence with logical reasoning.

Reading Levels for Texts

Text	Reading Level	Page
"My Maiden Voyage" by Roberta Maioni	6.5	18
"Should Fidget Spinners Be Banned from Schools?" by Jay Heller	7.6	20
"Namesake" by Greg Button	4.9	22
"A Long Lost Hero" by T. Robert Hall	5.7	23
"Lost in Translation" by Woody Blaine	6.1	25
"Up Close and Personal" by Charity Brinkley	5.3	26
"Khufu's Tomb" by Jack Williams	5.6	28
"The Dragon Jewel (A Japanese Myth)" by Oliver Kellog	6.1	29
"Fall Leaves Fall" by Emily Bronte	2.8	31
"Young and Old" by Charles Kingsley	2.6	32
"Mars Mission Application"	6.5	35
"DIY: Homemade Fireworks" by Izzy Tayler	5.6	39
Excerpt from "Dr. Martin Luther King Jr." by Gina Jefe	6.8	43
"Race the Wind" by Jesse Aaron	5.6	47
"The Golden Age—from *Old Greek Stories*" by James Baldwin	5.6	51
Excerpt from "The Bread Book"	5.7	55
"Waiting and Watching" by Charles Victor	6.1	59
Excerpt from "Sound Waves and Communication" by Bill Shrill	6.0	63
"Tell Me Again, Dad" by John K. Wayne	5.9	67
"The Nutrient Cycle" by Bob Nye	6.5	71
"Should Bottle Flipping be Considered a Sport?"	8.5	79
"Should Graffiti be Considered Art?"	8.9	80
"A Fork in Time" by Skyler Jack	6.4	91
"The Writing on the Wall" by Cesar Brady	6.1	94
"A Smart Move" by Jakob Taylor	6.7	97
"Win or Lose?" by Kate Wesson	6.4	100
"Cracking the Color Wheel" by Lisa Pennington	6.7	103
"Peanuts—A Potential Hazard" by Erik Charles	6.5	106
"Racing Rocks" by Valeria Yahir	6.4	109
"Super-Tasters" by Marty Remington	6.4	112
"Do You Hear What I Hear? by Carol Hansen	6.4	115
"A Royal Pastime" by Bryan Vega	6.5	118

Contents of the Digital Resources

To access the digital resources, go to this website and enter the following code: **74630717**

www.teachercreatedmaterials.com/administrators/download-files/

The contents of the digital resources is divided into two folders. Below are brief descriptions of each folder's contents.

Student Resources

This folder contains student reproducibles needed for the lessons. The filenames of these pages are included in the materials lists within the lessons. This folder also contains additional student resources, such as the charts and information from the appendices.

Teacher Resources

This folder contains the example student reproducibles. The filenames of these pages are included in the materials lists within the lessons. This folder also contains additional teacher resources, such as the charts and information from the appendices.

References Cited

Atkins, Janet. 2011. "From the Secondary Section: Reading and Writing with Purpose: In and Out of School." *The English Journal* 101(2): 12–13.

Fisher, Douglas B., and Nancy Frey. 2014. *Close Reading and Writing From Sources*. Newark, DE: International Reading Association.

Graham, Steve, and Michael Hebert. 2010. *Writing to Read: Evidence for How Writing Can Improve Reading.* A Carnegie Corporation Time to Act Report. Washington, DC: Alliance for Excellent Education.

CPSIA information can be obtained
at www.ICGtesting.com
Printed in the USA
LVHW020353230620
658710LV00012B/793

9 781425 817015